THE
PRIMARY ROUTE:

How the 99% Take On the Military Industrial Complex

A pamphlet

by Tom Gallagher

For George McGovern, the magnitude of whose achievement has never been fully appreciated.

CONTENTS

coasttocoastpublications.org
Boston, New York, San Francisco
ISBN #: 978-0-9916695-1-6:

The Primary Route – 2019

Would active participation in the presidential primary race advance the development of a serious American electoral left? Before 2016, the jury was out on this question. The argument for involvement in the presidential process was that, while success might be more likely in House or Senate races (and certainly in state or local races), a presidential candidacy offered a breadth of opportunity that the lower level races simply did not. Only the presidential election process provides a political forum involving the entire nation – a debate and discussion about where the country is at and where it wants to go, whose importance far surpasses that of any other event in the normal American political cycle. And the argument for participation specifically in the primaries (and caucuses) – as opposed to a "third party" run – rests on the fact that the primaries offer a "safe" option, a situation where candidates of the left are less likely to see their message overshadowed by the perceived danger of their efforts ultimately making matters worse by inadvertently helping to elect a Republican – a debate that has continued for nearly twenty years since Ralph Nader's 2000 run. After the Bernie Sanders campaign, the question of the value of taking the primary route would appear to be settled.

In the process of taking some unusually "big issues" – universal health insurance, a minimum wage that is actually a living wage, the history of U.S. overthrows of democratically elected governments, etc. – right into America's living rooms in the debates, the Sanders campaign arguably revolutionized the entire process, and certainly offered much of the country its first taste of "democratic socialism," that is "democratic socialism" as defined by a friend rather than a foe. The national political debate now included a perspective known throughout virtually all of the free world – but previously not here.

The question of the moment is whether this breakthrough will ultimately prove to be just a one-off historical anomaly or the beginning of a lasting sea change in American politics. Will the future include an American left consistently able to navigate the often murky challenges of real world politics? Or does it fall back to its traditional, largely non-participant critique, generally delivered from the margins?

To the extent that one needs to understand the past in order to plan the future, an accurate assessment of the Sanders campaign seems a prerequisite for any thoughtful advance planning And yet, maybe it's because the election of Donald Trump followed so close on the heels of Sanders's run and plunged us into a daily routine of shaking our heads and/or fists at the administration's latest outrages and follies, but it's not always totally clear whether the magnitude of the Sanders campaign achievement has really ever fully sunken in. (And the fact that he is again a candidate will only make dispassionate assessment of his last run all the more difficult.)

Simply put, in winning better than 13 million votes in the Democratic presidential primaries and caucuses, Bernie Sanders surpassed the combined vote total of every socialist presidential candidate in the prior history of the country. And yet we still find, on the one hand, self-identified socialists who consider the campaign to have been a failure or a diversion and, on the other, activists and advocates for many of the same causes the campaign championed who appear oblivious or indifferent to its remarkable success in promoting those issues.

It's difficult to say how many people fall into either of these groups – one suspects that the relatively unimpressed outnumber the actively opposed – but regardless of their sizes, the difficulty and urgency of actually enacting the sort of changes the Sanders campaign moved to the front burner suggest that there's some value in trying to get all of us who are trying to get to the same place onto the same train.

One strand of thought among the Sanders campaign's rejectionist opposition simply has it that the ultimate failure to win the nomination demonstrates the futility of the entire venture – we could and should have been doing something better with our time. Another argument faults Sanders for operating within the realm of the Democratic Party and, in doing so, validating the Wall Street types who dominate it, along with their interests and positions, positions that often run antithetical to his – and ours. Yet another viewpoint argues that the people who run the Democratic Party don't even want us there, so why should we stay where we're not wanted? Tying them all together is usually a belief that the situation calls for a "third party," a party of our own, a party that unambiguously shares his/our politics, a party that we control.

Unfortunately, history suggests that if we wanted a roadmap for a return to the marginality in which the American Left has so long labored, this would be pretty close to being it. Perhaps the most profoundly un- or even anti-political of these arguments is the idea that we ought to leave the Democratic Party because its powers-that-be don't like us. If we can't handle the fact that when you try to topple people from their positions of power they don't like it, we might want to consider devoting our energies to something other than politics. You want to contest for real power? Then expect pushback. These guys know what they're doing. And the fact that they want us gone is precisely the reason we need to stay: The Democratic Party represents a proven route to power. Specifically, the Democratic nominee has not finished out of the top two in a presidential race since the party's inception in 1828.

What does a third party option offer? Clarity? Yes, it is true that the creation of yet another new party on the left would enable a certain clarity of message beyond anything we're likely to achieve in the Democratic Party in the foreseeable future. But the question is who would listen to that clear message in the midst of the realities of the system in which we actually live? A lot of people who study such things will argue the virtues of a parliamentary system, one which allows for fielding candidates running on a distinct party program, after which, absent any party achieving an outright majority – a routine outcome in many parliamentary systems – the various parties have the option of combining with the party or parties closest to them in order to form a government, in opposition to the parties with which they have the least in common. If the U.S. had such a system in 2016, we might imagine Sanders and Clinton backers combining forces against Trump supporters and other hard right elements, forming a government and choosing a prime minister from the larger group to preside over it.

But, for better or worse, we don't live in such an "additive" system that allows the strengths of different parties to be combined after the voting is done – and we can't just wish it so. In the American reality, a new third party of the left might very well conduct a unified convention, create a coherent platform and select an articulate presidential candidate to run on that platform. And afterwards? History unfortunately suggests that said candidate would be doing very well to get even as much as three percent of the vote. The last "third party" presidential candidate of the left to reach even that level was Eugene Debs in 1920. (Robert LaFollette also did it in 1924, but he was actually a Republican – yes, there was such a thing as a left-wing Republican in those days.) And if the past be any guide, one thing our imagined candidate would likely win a lot of is – blame. For in the "subtractive" system used in American presidential elections, any third party offering an alternative to the candidate whom its backers might consider the "lesser of two evils" runs the risk of assisting in the election of the greater of the two evils. We just have to imagine the reaction to Trump being reelected in 2020 by electoral votes from states where his edge over the Democratic nominee was smaller than the number of votes cast for a prominent third party candidate of the left, in order to realize the potential for disaster in such a candidacy. Third parties can claim their share of accomplishments, to be sure. And there are electoral arenas in which they can and do thrive – but the presidential level is not one of them.

The failure to acknowledge the significance of the 2016 Sanders campaign is not limited to die-hard third party proponents, though. At the other edge, there appear to be a significant number of people who seemed to fit the profile of Sanders backers, but actually were not – including some leftists of longstanding, many even self-identified socialists. Some of them were wrong-footed by Sanders's entry into the race, having taken the Clinton nomination for a fait accompli, and/or assuming that Sanders had little electoral potential. For others, the prospect of electing the first female president outweighed the fact that they were otherwise closer to Sanders on the issues. Some may have had specific problems with Sanders as a candidate, a potential stumbling block with any candidate, who, unlike a bill or a ballot question, comes with a specific history and characteristics. Some may have thought, "He should be a Democrat," or "I didn't like that thing he did back when he was mayor of Burlington," etc. And some may simply have gotten so used to the prospect of choosing from a list of the best available Wall Street-oriented Democrats, that they were no longer able to recognize a candidate of a genuinely different stripe when the real thing finally came along.

There's no telling how large this group actually is, but it would appear to include a fair number of "movement types" who had dug in over the years in left-related activities in areas like fundraising, foundations, social services, advertising, public relations, legal work, journalism, and a few other professions. Whether or not they still consider going with Clinton the right thing to have done under the circumstances is, at this point, a matter of only personal significance. What does matter, however, is whether that past decision is even now blocking their recognition of the degree to which the Sanders campaign changed things – toward ends for which they had long labored. There is no real way to know either the answer to this question or the number of people involved, but the field of journalism, the most public of these professions, suggests there may be a substantial number who have yet to reassess the situation. Consider how many writers wax eloquent over the virtues of Alexandria Ocasio Cortez, but did no such thing in the case of Sanders in 16, and have given no indication of having reassessed their stance, seemingly ignoring, or remaining oblivious to how very unlikely it would have been for her to become the youngest woman ever elected to the U.S. Congress, absent the Sanders campaign.

Where does this all leave us, then? Early 2019 presents a vista of American politics unimaginable at the start of 2016. The starkest reality is a White House occupied by a man routinely referred to as a liar, presiding over the further enrichment of the already rich, the devastation of environmental regulation, and the poisoning of public discourse regarding those not of his race and gender; a man whose unprecedentedly outrageous behavior has shocked millions of us – every single day of his administration. On the other hand, we see an America potentially on the verge of a paradigm shift also without precedent, an America with a growing recognition that the earth's clock is ticking, a recognition that the people of this nation and this planet can no longer leave their destiny in the hands of profit-seeking corporations and the power-seeking military industrial complex, a recognition of the need to find the way to take that power into our own, democratic hands.

Next year's primaries and caucuses will again undoubtedly be a time of dispute and disagreement – that's what they're for. But for the first time in the lives of many, if not most, of the participating voters, there seems a realistic possibility of finishing this primary season with a candidate who not only surpasses the exceedingly low hurdle of being better than the current occupant of the White House, but one who is actually up to the challenge of establishing democratic control over the forces currently leading us down the road to ruin.

Preface

"The true pamphlet ... is a special literary form which has persisted without radical change for hundreds of years, though it has had its good periods and its bad ones. It is worth defining it carefully, even at the risk of seeming pedantic. It is written because there is something that one wants to say now, and because one believes there is no other way of getting a hearing."

George Orwell, *Introduction to British Pamphleteers Vol.1: From the 16th Century to the French Revolution*

Preface: *The Primary Route* and the Bernie Sanders Campaign

The Primary Route fits entirely within the category of political pamphlet that George Orwell describes, in that it is a book advocating a particular course of action: that those of us interested in creating a radically fairer and more just America need to take our case into the presidential primaries. Bernie Sanders has now taken that step as a candidate. It remains for the rest of us to seize the opportunity to change the terrain of political debate in this country permanently.

While this book has exerted no sway over Sanders's course of action, it makes the case for the rest of us, covering the same history and politics that Sanders considered. *The Primary Route* runs through a century and a half of third party presidential candidates and a century of presidential primaries; the conventions and platforms; and the labor movement and social issues along the way. It deals with the specifics of the American electoral system, along with that of several European countries as well. It may, then, clarify for some just how Sanders, who has so famously been *not*

The Primary Route

a Democrat for so long, might come to conclude that in running for president, he should take the primary rather than the third party route.

Presidential campaigns are long and treacherous trips and there's obviously no telling exactly how things may turn out with this one. Presumably there will be times along that campaign trail when the reader, like this writer, will disagree with one or another statement Sanders makes or some position he takes. This is inevitable when we reach past our individual political philosophy and deal with actual politics, and other people. But to the extent that the Sanders campaign pushes forward an agenda of delivering government from the grip of the few to the hands of the many, it will be doing precisely what this book argues needs to be done.

The Primary Route's argument for 2016 is that those of us who believe America needs to shift direction from permanent warfare footing to developing a sustainable economy that more widely shares the nation's wealth need to devote our attention to what could be the most sweeping debate we've seen in decades, as we master the political processes that are a part of it.

The Primary Route's argument for 2020, and every subsequent year divisible by four, is that we need to make sure that this point of view never again leaves the center stage of American political debate.

Introduction: The Primary Route

If you consider the following statements to be true:

America suffers from too great a concentration of wealth and power.

Our permanent war economy is not bringing us closer to genuine "national security."

We are currently frittering away our opportunities to develop energy sources that won't further degrade the planet.

And if you also think that most of what you find in mainstream politics fails to adequately address all of this, then I wrote this book with you in mind. I hope that you'll read on.

Occupy the Democratic Party?

This book originated in a brief conversation held one February evening on the steps outside the San Francisco Unitarian Universalist Center. I had just participated in a panel discussion inside. Organized by a local Occupy movement-inspired group, the panel had addressed the general question, "Which Way Forward?" For my part, I had argued that one valuable thing to do would have been to run someone against President Obama in the Democratic primaries. Unfortunately, the 2012 primary season had already begun, so it was actually already too late in the game to do much that might affect that year's presidential election – at least in any positive way. This was not a message that all that many people in the crowd that night had wanted to hear.

I'd argued three points that night:

13

The Primary Route

1. The question of who won the White House was a matter of great importance to a lot of people.

2. If we hoped to have a positive impact on the outcome of the race for the White House, the structure of the American presidential election system was such that we needed to participate in one of the two "major" parties – whether we liked it or not and regardless of whether or not we loved either of those two parties.

3. However far they might be from the ideals of the people in the room, the fact was that the Democrats were better than the Republicans.

One of the other speakers on the panel was an actual presidential candidate. And he had a legitimate electoral record: Rocky Anderson was a past two-term Democratic mayor of Salt Lake City who had now opted to seek the presidency on the Justice Party ticket. So while I had essentially only been able to offer regrets that we had probably already missed our opportunity, he at least had offered the crowd the prospect of doing *something* by supporting his campaign.

I'd empathized with the goals of his campaign and explained that I sorely wished that someone had gotten it together to challenge Obama from the left in the Democratic primaries – and from what I heard that night it actually sounded like Rocky Anderson would have filled that bill just fine, had he chosen to take that route. But the fact was that right now, as primary season was beginning, the only discernable challenge to Obama's continuing Afghanistan War, the bombing – via plane or drone – of four additional Muslim countries, and all the rest was coming from Ron Paul. Paul, however, was a libertarian who was running in the *Republican* primaries and also had views on various domestic social policies that would make most of the people in that room gag.

Unfortunately, then, it was already time to start thinking about what we could do in the *next* presidential election, i.e., 2016. I also did muse aloud about how we could have used all of those fierce Obama critics so vocally present in tonight's crowd, back when Dennis Kucinich was trying to run against Obama in the 2008 presidential primaries. And we could have used them even more when Kucinich ran the first time in the 2004 primaries.

And while it gave me no pleasure to dis Rocky Anderson, who appeared to have a fine platform, I pointed out to the crowd that it seemed pretty clear that right now there was not a lot of support on the left for another third party presidential campaign. For the fact was, regardless of how one apportioned the "blame" for George W. Bush's election in 2000, there was virtually no measure by which Ralph Nader's campaign that year could be deemed to have been a success – and there just weren't a lot of people ready to look in that direction again.

I suspected that Obama had actually broken a lot of hearts in that room. And that the crowd that night might have included more than a few who hadn't really listened all that closely to much of what Obama had actually campaigned on four years earlier – perhaps in deference to their feelings about how important it was that he be elected. But whatever the reasons, it was a fact that there were a lot of people there in the church that night who just didn't want to hear anything about how they couldn't get back at him come November – at least not in any constructive way.

(Anderson proved not to offer much of a real option, by the way: The Justice Party failed to gain a slot on the California ballot and he received 86 write-in votes in San Francisco.)

As I awaited a ride home after the event, I ran into Karl, an economist of my acquaintance, who told me that he could accept the argument I'd been making inside – were it not for the fact that it had already been tried so often. Well, I started to explain that what I actually had in mind – a permanent left presence in the presidential primaries, continuing from one election to the next – had really *never* been tried. But then my ride came, leaving me thinking that if a person like Karl – whom I considered both knowledgeable and sensible, based on a talk he'd given to our local Progressive Democrats of America chapter – didn't really follow my argument, then maybe I ought to write this book to explain it at some length.

The Primary Route

Certainly I hadn't gotten all that far along on the details that night. My first and third points were straightforward enough, I figured. Presumably the crowd agreed that the presidency was an immensely important institution – they wouldn't have been all that upset with Obama if they didn't. And, much as many of them might have been in a foot-stomping, plague-on-both-your-houses mood that night, I was also pretty sure that not a one of them had voted for John McCain four years earlier, and that none of them would be voting for the eventual Republican nominee (Mitt Romney) that November either. But I understood that my second point, about how to approach the presidency in our actually existing political system, is an argument that can take some time to develop.

One of the ways in which the U.S. remains an "exceptional" nation is that it is virtually unique among the world's reasonably democratic, industrialized countries in not having an electoral left, that is, a party or faction that consistently espouses the cause of the nation's working class, as opposed to deferring to or siding with its corporate interests. As a result, when the country holds its national presidential debate every four years, the point of view sketched out on the first page of this book is generally nowhere to be found. The conventional understanding of the cause for this anomaly is that the absence of an American left is a byproduct of our country's "two-party system," where a vote for the best candidate may carry the risk of getting you the worst winner. While I didn't dispute that there was something of a cause-effect relationship here, I had been arguing that there was a "work-around" available and that this "work-around" was not simply an option, but a necessity. A necessity, that is, if we wished our viewpoint to be taken seriously in national politics.

In short, I was claiming that the route to relevance that has so long eluded the American left was essentially hiding in plain sight – in the form of the presidential primaries. But at the same time, I did of course understand that although my argument might seem uncomplicated, this simple "answer" couldn't have stayed hidden for all this time if it really was all that simple. The fact was that the American left's view of how – and even *if* – it should participate in the presidential election process was clouded by a

Introduction

century of disappointments, misperceptions and wishful thinking. Looking back, I might ask how I could have ever realistically hoped that a series of intermittent remarks made in the middle of a panel discussion could cut through the Gordian Knot of all of that encrusted history.

If it's possible to speak of something "sneaking up" on a nation over a period of a hundred years, then that's exactly what the presidential primaries have done. Arriving with something of a splash in 1912, their significance has grown immensely, but this development has been unsteady and intermittent. When they first reached something like their current level of importance – in 1972 – they produced what was arguably the American left's greatest electoral achievement – the nomination of George McGovern as the Democrats' presidential candidate. Unfortunately, the magnitude of this achievement was seemingly lost in the magnitude of McGovern's subsequent loss to incumbent President Richard Nixon in November of that year. And certainly, while the cause may be debatable, few would argue anything but that the American left has subsequently never returned to the presidential primaries with anything like the same force and determination it demonstrated that year.

Jesse Jackson, Ralph Nader and Dennis Kucinich walk into a bar

At one point this book's working title was *Occupy the Democratic Party*. I'd actually suggested to the crowd attending the "Which Way Forward?" event that "occupying" the Democratic Party might be the way for them to think about getting involved in the presidential election process – since I knew that a lot of people in the audience would probably only consider getting involved in the Democratic Party if they thought that their doing so would really annoy the top Democrats.

With the fading of the Occupy movement, I then thought of somehow getting Jesse Jackson, Ralph Nader and Dennis Kucinich into the title, since it was their presidential campaigns that really provided the long-term impetus for this book. For a brief time, Jesse Jackson's two primary runs – in 1984 and particularly in

The Primary Route

1988 – looked like they might actually be creating something you could legitimately consider an American electoral left. For brief stretches, views usually heard only on the fringes of American political discussion became the stuff of the nightly news – so long as Jackson was a factor in the debates.

But then no one emerged who proved capable of picking up the baton from Jackson in the next two presidential election cycles. And when Ralph Nader decided to make the race as a third party candidate in 2000, the results wound up pleasing virtually no one on the left side of the political fence – neither among Nader's supporters nor his detractors – as George W. Bush won the presidency while the Nader campaign did not succeed in leaving behind any alternative movement or structures. Yet when Dennis Kucinich arrived on the scene to attempt to pick up the pieces and bring the race back into the Democratic primaries in 2004 and 2008 – where no one might accuse him of helping to elect a Republican president – very few proved willing to follow.

Most people sympathetic to Kucinich's politics found that the prospect of his actually taking the nomination simply did not seem like a realistic possibility. This, of course, had also been the situation with the Jackson campaign. But where substantial numbers went ahead and voted for Jackson anyway, most of Kucinich's potential base appeared to conclude that they would be somehow wasting their votes if they gave them to him. And with that shift in perception went any lingering belief or hope that some vestige of an American electoral left had survived on the national level.

This book has been germinating since that first Kucinich campaign. Looking backward, it is, of course, an argument that the people who actually agreed with Kucinich in 2004 should have voted for him and helped build his campaign. But if it were only that, I would have let it go as the stuff of barroom discussions, real or imagined. The real argument here is about the future. It's an argument that we *always* need presidential candidates saying the sorts of things Kucinich did – win or lose. And we have to *vote* for them, support them and *work* for them – every time. And, crucially, it is an argument that these candidates should run in the primaries

Introduction

where we might be able to take advantage of the element of "additive" coalition-building potential, an element that does not exist in the final election itself.[1]

This book makes no claim to predicting the future. There is no claim herein that what this book argues *should* happen necessarily *will* happen. Nor does it come with any kind of implicit guarantee. It does not purport to promise that if we will only follow its prescribed course of action we are guaranteed success in steering the course of national politics toward a direction we'd rather see it go. This book simply argues that if we – the people who think the U.S. needs to spend more money on helping people at home and less on waging war abroad – are really serious about breaking with our legacy of mostly watching the country's main political events from the sidelines, we have to use the openings *that actually exist* in the electoral system *that actually exists* – and not imagine that we can simply wish some other better system into existence or wait for it to happen.

This book is not intended as any kind of political "theory of everything." It does not argue that the one and only thing we need to do to profoundly change the course of American politics is to make a more serious commitment to the presidential race. As a logical proposition, we might say that what this book advocates is conceived of as being *necessary, but not sufficient.* The list of ways in which we might go about trying to change this country for the better is a long one – but this is definitely on it.

Nor does this book maintain that all who read it need to drop everything else and throw themselves into the presidential race every four years. It does argue, however, that any of us who are seriously interested in redirecting our politics do need to give the presidential election, and specifically the primaries, serious consideration every four years, and that at least some of us have to figure out how to make the candidacies that will run on those issues actually materialize.

Success, we know, can never be guaranteed. But unfortunately failure can be. And this book *does* argue that, until and unless we do learn how to constructively engage in the nation's presidential selection process, all of our ideas on reorienting our

19

The Primary Route

national economic system, our foreign policy, our energy development, and all the rest, are *guaranteed* to remain marginal – no matter how brilliant they may be.

The American Left: Do We Exist?

To be or not to be? The American left's Hamlet complex

This book is all about a simple argument that a group of people that I'm rather generically calling the American left absolutely has to figure out how to work its way into presidential politics if it means to be taken seriously. By the "American left," I simply mean those of us who would like to see our government demilitarize our foreign policy and direct the nation's considerable resources toward tasks like developing a sustainable energy economy; or expanding our social safety net, particularly with a universal access health care system like every other industrialized nation already has; or reversing the growing disparity of wealth; or reducing the political influence of corporations.

This group, as I conceive of it, encompasses a wide range of people. Some of them might consider themselves "liberals," some "progressives," some "socialists." Many may not think distinctions like "liberal/conservative" or "left/right" mean much of anything at all. Some may bristle about being labeled as "left." (Any title or description comes with connotations, some of them unwanted, but I saw little point in trying to conjure up a brand new connotation-free name just for this book.) Naturally, no two people in this book's target audience will actually think exactly alike. There will always be specific issues on which individuals will disagree vehemently, even when they hold the same general views. So although this author has his own set of strongly held opinions on the issues of the day, which will inevitably differ in some particulars from those of various readers, for the most part those opinions will not find their way into this book. If you're looking for specifics on Middle East politics, for instance, you won't find them here. In fact, the only position this book really

21

argues (in addition to the central argument on the presidential primaries) is the necessity of emphasizing the broad range of similar views that unite the American left (by whatever name the reader prefers), rather than highlighting the ones that may divide us.

If the general run of thinking on the first page of this book's introduction fits you, then I hope you'll read on. That short list will understandably strike some as pretty sketchy but nevertheless, if you'll just compare it to the platforms of the traditional mainstream presidential contenders, you'll quickly see that, bare bones as it is, it does describe a "left" point of view that is generally shut out of the national debate.

The people who fit my conception of "the left" may not constitute a majority of the electorate at any particular moment, but they are by no means a small group. By some measures you'd probably have to estimate their ranks in the tens of millions. Yet by other standards, the group doesn't exist at all. And that's the reason for this book.

The Primary Route's central premise is that the quadrennial presidential election process constitutes America's most important arena of political debate. If a viewpoint isn't somehow involved in that election process, it's simply not a factor in the national debate. So due to our usual absence from that arena, "non-factor" pretty well describes the current situation of those of us holding the political views that were roughly scratched out above. And while active participation in the presidential election process does not guarantee that we will actually develop into what the rest of the world might recognize as a (heretofore absent) American electoral left, our failure to engage in those events will guarantee us a permanent place on the sidelines.

The re-election of a president generally sets off a particular type of political soul searching. After four years everyone now pretty much knows what to expect for the next four and can set their stances and expectations in a way they couldn't four years earlier. Barack Obama's re-election in 2012

provided such a moment. So far as the American left went, no wild optimism greeted the event, to be sure, but it certainly seemed

The American Left: Do We Exist?

better than the prospect of four more years of George W. Bush had eight years earlier.

One particularly noticeable product of the reflection process triggered by the Obama re-election was a plethora of To-Do-Over-the-Next-Four-Years lists for the American left. These lists had no shortage of good ideas about the issues mentioned above, along with things like building progressive state organizations, developing a culture of organizing and much more. Absent from those lists though, was finding or developing 2016 presidential candidates of the left. So while there was ample discussion about the prospects of Hillary Clinton and Joe Biden, but not of identifying candidates who would actually take the sorts of priorities on the list makers' lists – priorities generally consistent with this book's broad brush categories – directly to the voters in the next presidential election. There was no mention of Bernie Sanders, or anyone like him, actually entering the fray. Sanders, like the intermittent contenders from the left before him, would have to take it on himself.

Not that this omission should surprise us. The last candidate to put together that type of campaign successfully was Jesse Jackson, back in 1988. Jackson's platform was a fair approximation of the left's To-Do List at that time. He advocated creation of a Works Progress Administration-style infrastructure program, a fifteen percent military budget cut, a single-payer universal health care system, extending free public education to the community college level, reversing tax cuts for the richest and earmarking the resulting revenue for social welfare programs, and even reparations to descendants of slaves. He won 1219 delegates with that program, just a hair under thirty percent of that year's Democratic Convention total. At the time, no one seemed to consider this anything but a reasonable approximation of his overall support among primary voters.

The Primary Route

In 1988, Jesse Jackson ran the last primary campaign to successfully raise the issues of the left in a presidential race.

And there it ended – for the next 24 years, anyway. My assumption here is that an American left – that is, voters who support the sorts of things Jackson ran on – has continued to exist during the nearly three decades since that campaign. And yet, over the course of the six Democratic nominating conventions held since 1988, the grand total of delegates won by candidates with platforms reflecting those positions is 64. And outside of the Democratic Party, there was Ralph Nader's 2000 campaign which different people call different things, none of which is successful. So what happened? In terms of carrying the ideas of the Jackson campaigns forward, the simple answer is about nothing. No candidate has since been able to effectively re-tap the base of support that Jackson tapped. And no significant movement has ever come together to try to make that happen.

You Know it Ain't Easy

There's not much mystery to any of this, though. Gathering support in an election that you don't have a reasonable expectation

The American Left: Do We Exist?

of winning always poses a high hurdle for a candidate. And most of the people who fit our definition of the American left simply haven't thought that someone can get elected president running on a platform based on the things that they believe. And in this assessment the left may be correct. At the same time, any political force that takes itself seriously enough to have long-run ambitions will obviously have to find a way to put its ideas in play before a broader public. And there is no better or more necessary way to do this than through the presidential primary process.

The fact is that while Jackson's campaigns may now look like the good old days when candidates "ran on the issues," Jackson himself ran in the face of serious skepticism. Since it was generally accepted that he was not going to be elected president, political commentators kept asking, "What does Jesse want?" The voters themselves, however, seemed to understand pretty well what Jesse wanted – because a lot of them wanted it too. Even if they weren't going to win, they wanted these ideas be part of the national political debate. As a result of that willingness to back someone who wasn't going to win, America heard more about the sorts of issues that were on Jackson's To-Do list in 1988 than it had in a long time. Some of the ideas he ran on hadn't made it back to center stage since.

Jackson, we know, brought a unique credential to his candidacy. As controversial a figure he was, his standing as a civil rights leader carried enough weight among African-American voters to allow him to immediately pass the mainstream media's laugh test. This, in turn, gave him access to an even larger audience. And by the second time around, Jackson did have a campaign organization that might have been modest compared to that of the better funded candidates but was far better developed than any left presidential candidate had mounted in some time. But when Jackson opted against a third run in 1992, there was no one like him to turn to. The most prominent figure to try to pick up the baton from Jackson was Larry Agran, past mayor of Irvine, California, a credential that proved insufficient to gain him entrance into the candidate debates – or to create any movement to assert his right to be there.

The Primary Route

Bill Clinton won it all that year and then faced no Democratic opposition four years later. Probably the memory of Ted Kennedy's 1980 challenge to Jimmy Carter and the sense that it had somehow contributed to Ronald Reagan's election played a role in Clinton's free ride among the Democrats in 1996. But then no candidate of Jackson's stripe emerged in the 2000 Democratic primaries either. That year Ralph Nader, who did have recognition and support that was arguably comparable to Jackson's and who had made a couple of desultory Democratic primary efforts in prior years, opted instead to run in the final election as the Green Party candidate, a candidacy that caused many to blame him for George W. Bush's election.

When Cleveland, Ohio, Representative Dennis Kucinich brought a candidacy of the left back to the Democratic primaries in 2004, the one-time boy wonder mayor of that city was certainly better known than Agran. Yet some still seemed to think it presumptuous for a House member with no leadership position to even run for president. Certainly he never caught on the way Jackson had – or even to the degree that Nader had – despite the similarity of their programs. Although his campaign would account for all of the Democratic convention delegates of the left elected since Jackson's second run, Kucinich's overall total primary vote represented nothing more than a small fraction of the voters who actually sympathized with him on the issues. The "he can't win" argument appeared to carry a lot more sway with primary voters – even among those who agreed with him – than the idea that there might be value in electing delegates who supported his/their positions. (Some may also consider Al Sharpton's 2004 candidacy as a campaign of the left, in which case his 20 delegates would raise the post-Jackson total to 84.)

Kucinich tried again next time around, but where Jackson's first run in 1984, which had netted him over 400 delegates, propelled him to greater things in1988, Kucinich's 2008 attempt went pretty much nowhere, as did former Alaska Senator Mike Gravel's candidacy run on a very similar set of issues. So, while the lack of a challenge to Barack Obama in 2012 was not unusual in the case of an incumbent president, at this point you had to wonder if this total absence from the presidential election proceedings hadn't really become the new normal for the American left.

Do We Exist?

In fact, we might ask if the left's continued non-participation in the country's central political arena refutes the idea that there actually is something we can call an "American left." To play devil's advocate on that, I'll suggest a thought experiment. For some real perspective on the question, we're not just going to look at the global picture – we're going to go interplanetary: Imagine, if you will, that there are scientists from another world monitoring our planet. These extraterrestrials are less like their planet's NASA (National Aeronautics and Space Administration) scientists than their planet's NSA (National Security Administration). They're political scientists – with broad listening capabilities. So where our earthly natural scientists search for biological life on other planets, our extraterrestrial scientists search for signs of political life.[2]

These listeners have gotten to the point, we'll imagine, where they've refined their study sufficiently so as not only to identify the different nations on earth but to start analyzing those nations' politics. Some countries, they've found, choose their governments in obscure, relatively private ways. Some have rulers who govern because their family always does. In others religious leaders call the shots. But the ones they find the most interesting are the ones that hold elections of some sort to select their government.

These elections have allowed our far-outside observers to draw up lists of all of the political forces that are legally operating in the various nations on earth, based upon their assumption that every political grouping that exists puts itself forward in national elections unless legally prevented from doing so. While the elections they study vary widely in both method and quality, nevertheless, they have allowed our onlookers to discern global patterns within them from which they could categorize the national political groupings they've encountered as "left," "center," or "right," based on their relative enthusiasm for government activity to promote social and economic

The Primary Route

Extraterrestrial political scientist searching for sign of American left.

equalization. One of the surprising conclusions that our researchers have reached is that in the country that currently seems to be the planet's most influential, there is no political left. They monitor one national election after the other and it while it may flare up once in awhile, it does not do so consistently. Evidence of its existence is not reproducible.

Back here on earth, in the U.S., where it can almost be considered impolite to accuse anyone of leaning in any direction except center, we're so used to this situation that it may not faze many people at all. What may matter to more people, though, is the silent treatment that some of our most important issues receive during our presidential campaigns which – it says here, anyhow – are our most important national discussions. Consider the Afghanistan War during the 2012 election. Despite polls showing great majorities now believing that the now decade-long war had not been worth fighting and had not made the U.S. any safer, during the presidential campaign the only arguments you heard against continuing it came from Texas Congressman Ron Paul, who ran in the *Republican* primaries. This was pretty much the case with the illegal bombing of Pakistan – and other countries – and even the matter of the entire enormous military industrial

28

complex in general. A lot of what Paul had to say about those issues was excellent, but since these views floated in a sea of other positions that were anathema to most people who might agree with his foreign policy, his candidacy was of little use in fostering an antiwar movement.

A year-end *New York Times* headline summed it up: "Among Top News Stories, a War Is Missing." [3] The paper reported that the Pew Research Center, the Associated Press and Yahoo all failed to list "the 11-year-old war in Afghanistan and American-led counterterrorism efforts around the world" among 2012's top stories. 68,000 American troops still deployed in our longest war ever – and it wasn't an issue in a presidential campaign. But no one said it was – or at any rate no one who could be heard.

Or take health care: If you were hoping to hear anything of the case for how much more sense a "Medicare-for-all," "single-payer," nonprofit health insurance system would make in contrast to the Affordable Health Care Act, then 2012 was not your year either, despite the fact that 78 members of the House of Representatives were co-sponsoring legislation to do precisely that. Instead, the only critique of "Obamacare" articulated at all in 2012 came from the right, which denounced it as socialism, an unwarranted federal government intrusion into the free market of private, for-profit health insurance.

These two obvious questions were only the tip of a much larger iceberg of issues that remained largely submerged throughout a presidential election season, when you might never have guessed that there were people who thought banks or energy companies needed to be more strictly regulated. Full employment as a goal? You never heard about it. The government leading the way to a non-fossil fuel energy future? Nope, not much of that either.

The effects of these presidential campaign issues blackouts are not confined to the nation's capital, either. In California, for instance, 2013 was the first time in ten years that there was no single-payer bill filed in the state Legislature. First introduced by Senator Sheila Kuehl[4] a decade earlier, the bill had twice passed both branches only to be vetoed by Republican Governor Arnold

The Primary Route

Schwarzenegger. Yet not one of 27 Democratic Senators or 48 Assembly Members (a two-thirds majority in both houses) would sponsor the bill in 2013. Given its recent past level of support, it's difficult to imagine that this bill could have been "disappeared" so easily, had the idea not suffered a total national blackout in the prior year's presidential race. But what is – and is not – debated on the national level profoundly affects discussion all the way down to the city council and town meeting level.

How much we think any of this matters probably depends upon what we think politics is all about. Despite our usual lack of a horse in the presidential race, our views on what the government ought to be doing with our money are still out there. The arguments the Jackson platform once brought to the nightly news are certainly still being discussed beyond college seminar rooms. Plus, the Internet is now available for leftists (as well as rightists and centrists) of all stripes to promote their take on things, so there's no shortage of critique or good ideas. For some, that may be enough. There are those, after all, who think that electoral politics is tainted by its very nature.

But if politics implies action, then our absence from mainstream debate is a serious shortcoming – maybe our most serious. If it's truly the case that not being part of the solution is tantamount to being part of the problem, then so far as the presidential debate goes, we're part of the problem. In short, if we actually hope to take on the banking industry, the for-profit health insurance business or the military-industrial boondoggle, someone has got to articulate these ideas in our presidential election campaigns. And for that to happen we need to start asking where the candidates to raise the issues are going to come from, each and every time. To be sure, left wing presidential candidacies will not in themselves be sufficient to bring about the type of changes the candidates would advocate, but it is impossible to even imagine such changes occurring in the absence of those national campaigns.

What Do We Know? Additive and Subtractive Political Systems

The closer we look at our history, the harder it becomes to avoid the conclusion that we on the American left have simply never mastered the system that we *actually* live in. Some of the operative misperceptions of the past have been spectacularly off-base – there's the absurd/tragic stories of groups like the Weathermen or the various revolutionary parties structured for operating in a czarist dictatorship. More common, though, have been those who quietly despaired at their ability to ever affect American politics and simply concluded that the best they could do was to try to keep the American military from destroying someone else's revolution. And as for the history of the actual forays the American left has made into national politics, it may bring to mind the tale of the donkey caught between the two bales of hay who can't decide which one to turn to and as a result goes nowhere and starves – the American left's two bales being the Democratic Party and a succession of third parties. There have been moves in both directions, but the simple fact is that we have never fully committed to either. As far as electoral politics goes, just like that donkey, we are still nowhere – well into the twenty-first century.

There's a reason for our historic confusion of course – each of those political hay bales has something we wish the other had. This does not, however, make the respective advantages of the two options equal. On the one side, the third party route, at this point meaning anything but the Democratic and Republican parties, does have one immensely appealing aspect – it offers the prospect of clarity: the more parties one has to choose from, the greater your chance of finding one you strongly agree with, as opposed to

The Primary Route

feeling stuck voting for a party or candidate you really only prefer by, say, only a 51-49 percent margin. And certainly the last couple of elections have involved substantial issues on which the positions of the Democratic and Republican presidential nominees seemed to offer only uninspiring choices. If, for instance, you were looking for an approach to the financial crisis that did not leave the powers of the banks intact, or you were looking for a candidate who thought the permanent threat of the use of nuclear weapons against Iran *wasn't* a perfectly legitimate element of foreign policy, well, you were out of luck. Such positions were simply not available in the Obama-McCain and Obama-Romney races. And there were any number of other major issues where neither candidate proposed a reasonable option.

Another thing that the third party idea has going for it is the undeniable fact of success stories in a variety of local and occasionally even statewide situations. The fact is that, considered as a whole, the United States has an immensely complex political system, with election laws that famously vary not only from state to state but even from county to county. In this vast multiplex, there are numerous locales where third parties can and have worked well. But it is precisely the fact that there are such drastic differences in American election processes – far more than is the case in most countries – that requires us to carefully assess each of them in its particulars. The considerations in selecting a mayor in a non-partisan municipal election can be quite different from the rules that obtain in electing a president.

Any number of people who've had the time and opportunity to compare political systems will tell you they'd prefer it if we in this country got to choose our government in a different manner. On the left I suspect that many wish lists would include adopting one or another type of parliamentary system that might allow for the creation of coalition governments. The fundamental aspect of a system of that type that's relevant to this discussion is that if your preferred party did not succeed in winning an outright majority and no other party did either, a quite routine occurrence in many parliamentary systems, it would have the option of combining forces with another party, perhaps your second-favorite party, and thereby potentially preventing your least-favorite party from controlling the government. An election system that embodies this characteristic I'm going to call an "additive process."

The "additive process" is extremely compelling. If we lived in circumstances where it was in play, an argument for a party to the left of the Democratic Party that could join forces with the Democrats in opposition to the Republicans, if need be, might make perfect sense. But the system we've actually got does not work that way at all. In the U.S.A. today, a vote for the third party on the left that you *really want* in a November presidential election always comes with the risk of increasing the chances of getting a president from a party that you *really don't want*. That is to say, to the extent that a candidate of a party of the left were to win votes that would otherwise have gone to the Democrat (because the Democrat might have been deemed the "lesser of two evils"), then all other things being equal, that candidate's vote would enhance the prospects of electing a Republican president. We might then describe the setup we've got in our presidential elections as a "subtractive process," a simple but profound difference that probably poses a permanent roadblock to third party presidential candidacies as an avenue for social change. The last big one, Ralph Nader's 2000 Green Party run, for instance started with great expectations, yet left nothing behind at the end – in part due to the widespread perception that it had helped tip the election to George W. Bush.

For some, however, the prospect of running a candidate of the left within the Democratic Party seems too murky a proposition. Want to know what the Green Party stands for? Google it. Want to know what the left wing of the Democratic Party stands for? Subscribe to five magazines and discuss. Engaging in the Democratic Party might mean supporting a great candidate all the way through the primaries and still ending up with that 51-49 candidate on election day. But while there's no denying the disadvantages of the primary route, the one very substantial advantage it does have is not running the risk of enhancing the prospects of the candidate you *really* don't want. The difference is crucial. Dennis Kucinich may have been ignored in his presidential runs, but no one ever claimed that he helped George W. Bush get elected.

It is also the case that the presidential primary process actually does embody the parliamentary system's ability to combine forces – although this factor has largely been forgotten as it has fallen into disuse in recent years. The fact is, though, that the contest for the presidential nomination is potentially an additive process. In this it differs not only from the actual presidential election in November but also from most other election processes in the nation. In 1988, as it turned out, Jackson's delegates weren't needed for Michael Dukakis to secure the Democratic presidential nomination, since they were the only two candidates still standing by the time of the convention. But given that three other candidates – Al Gore, Dick Gephardt and Paul Simon – had actually won a combined 11 primaries, it's easy to imagine a situation having developed that year in which no candidate did arrive at the convention with the necessary majority of committed delegates. In that case Jackson's delegates would have mattered. Any other candidates who wanted those delegates' second-ballot votes would then have had to make their case as to how and why they came closest to the political views that had brought the Jackson delegates to the convention. They might even have had to make concessions in the party's platform.

As we know, however, the actual trend has been entirely in the other direction, to the point where the very idea that there could even be a second ballot at a nominating convention is rarely discussed and many people may not be aware that such a possibility even exists. In fact, we've grown so accustomed to seeing one candidate wrap up the nomination before the convention that when Hillary Clinton seemed ready to pursue her candidacy right on into the 2008 convention, she was pilloried by Barack Obama supporters who acted as though doing so would constitute an act of disloyalty to the party. The fact that this line of attack met with pretty fair success seemed to reflect what has become an underlying assumption in today's elections that an also-ran candidate campaigning for the nomination too hard and too long would inevitably weaken the eventual nominee.

This was not always the case, though. The most successful

Additive And Subtractive Political Systems

presidential candidate in American history – Franklin Delano Roosevelt, who was elected four times – did not get his first nomination on the first ballot. In 1932, when nomination required two-thirds support instead of the current simple majority, it took FDR four ballots to win it before he went on to a landslide victory in November.

Clearly the idea of restoring some of the importance of nominating conventions after more than eighty years would be a tall order. And the drift toward media-driven conventions where a show of unity is all, and issues and platform are naught, has been relentless, to the point where even the idea of creating a issues-dominated campaign like Jackson's has often come to seem like too daunting a task. But the whole point of mounting presidential candidacies of the left is to reverse any number of trends that have come to dominate American society in recent years. So if we would seriously presume to challenge the legitimacy and control of the entire military industrial complex, surely we can undertake the task of assembling campaigns that are motivated by common interests and values rather than by image makers competing to spin the most compelling "narrative" about their candidates.

As we will surely observe in the Sanders campaign, nothing about the process of committing to such issues-based candidacies on the presidential level is likely to be simple or easy. Presidential primaries operate under a complex set of rules that require different calculations from state to state. Issue and delegate-based campaigns involve compromise and disagreement. They are messy. Then there's the possibility that if and when they achieve broader exposure, some of our favorite ideas may not sound so good as we might hope. Some of them may have to go back to the drawing board. But that is the stuff of actual, real-life politics – on the highest level. And in politics, no matter how good your theories may be, there is just no substitute for reality. To the extent that we're committed to change and not just to talk, it's not a matter of *if* we need to undertake serious engagement in the presidential process, but *how*.

The Primary Route

But How?

In recent tradition, running for President of the United States has been something of an entrepreneurial endeavor, the Sanders campaign being no exception to that rule. Candidates surface and then go off seeking support, organization, money and, ultimately, votes. They're cultivated by various groups and organizations along the way, of course, but there is no recognized forum for choosing them, save the party nominating convention itself. All of which means that if we want to be in the game in the future, we need to be looking and listening for candidates *now*. Who knows – there could even be more than one candidate of the left who thinks that he or she is *the one*. And two or more national figures calling for major change at the same time would not necessarily be the worst thing – the worst thing is having none. We might even imagine that the competition could offer added impetus for the rest of us to get out there to back one of them or the other.

The more likely prospect, though, is having too few candidates of the left, which is to say less than one, although, at the risk of losing any mainline Democratic "party regulars" who've stuck with me thus far, I'll point out that it was Ralph Nader who suggested a way of dealing with a situation when there simply wasn't a candidate willing and/or able to run a national campaign. His idea was to revive the tradition of running favorite sons or daughters, seeking out simpatico candidates to run campaigns in a single state or region and thereby separately elect delegates who might hook up at the national convention.

Eventually, we could imagine, or at least hope, that if presidential candidacies of the left were ever to become a routine and expected thing, the ad hoc, self-selecting aspect of the current nominating process might come to be seen as insufficiently democratic. We might envision a desire for something of a more participatory candidate selection process down the road, perhaps some form of organization that could maintain a measure of continuity from one presidential election cycle to the next. But that would be getting ahead of ourselves right now when we're not nearly well organized enough to even imagine having such problems. First we need to start considering the presidential

Additive And Subtractive Political Systems

primary process as a serious undertaking, with each campaign more or less putting it together from scratch.

Like any other area of political activity, presidential politics cannot make an exclusive claim on our time and effort. Big a deal as a presidential election may be, it is also the fact that it is an intermittent, one-every-four-years event that by no means encompasses the full range of political activity that circumstances call for, even on the electoral level alone. Recognizing the importance of involvement in presidential politics in no way diminishes the need for campaigns for Congress, the State House or City Hall. Beyond that, a presidential campaign, no matter how well conducted, can never fill our ongoing need for a revived labor movement. Likewise, the political void that the "Occupy" movement filled, however briefly or ephemerally, will still be there, even if we should see a substantial uptick in the quality of White House campaigns from the left. And no matter how good our future campaigners might be, they will continue to find their efforts diminished at every turn unless the corrosive effect of big money on government is limited through campaign finance or electoral reforms. But while the list of other things that need to be done in addition to presidential campaigning is endless, an effective national campaign conducted on the principles of creating a more democratic, egalitarian economy can only enhance the prospects of success for similar efforts on the state or local level.

While the late Speaker of the House, Tip O'Neill of Massachusetts was quite right in his famous mantra that "All politics is local," the converse is no less true. All of our politics have a national dimension. Local and state level decisions are never made in isolation from the questions that dominate the national news. And no matter how remote they may seem at times, presidential elections and presidential politics are all of our business.

The Primary Route

The Third Party Route

Although the entire argument of this book is that the route to future presidential election relevance runs through the primaries rather than "third parties," the history of third parties is an essential part of the history of the American left. Just as third parties do have the advantage of being more easily definable than campaign efforts conducted within the Democratic Party, their story is more easily told. And the fact is that there is also much more of a story to be told here than there is of campaigns of the left within the Democratic Party.

This story runs through all of the substantial third party efforts mounted since 1832, before the Republican Party first moved into a top-two slot alongside the Democrats. With the Republicans nudging the Whigs off the top in 1856, for a considerable time afterwards other new parties quite logically continued to hope they themselves might similarly supplant either the Democrats or the Republicans. In hindsight, we may see the 1912 election as the pivotal point in the history of those efforts. Not only would it be the highpoint of independent presidential politics on the left, when Socialist Party candidate Eugene Debs got his best percentage of the vote of any of his five runs, but 56 years after the start of the Democratic/Republican duopoly, the Republicans were relegated to a third place finish when their former President Theodore Roosevelt formed his own party and beat their incumbent President William Taft. The Republicans immediately bounced back, however, and have never dropped from the top two again. Yet the third party strategy still seemed viable in 1924 when Wisconsin Senator Robert La Follette recorded the highest percentage of any third party presidential candidate we might consider to be running from the left. La

The Third Party Route

Follette carried his home state, gaining its electoral votes, which would prove to be the only ones a twentieth-century third party presidential candidate of the left would ever win.

It was another development introduced in the 1912 election, however, that would alter the course of presidential politics in a direction that would not be fully realized for some time. 1912 saw the introduction of the party presidential primary. The primaries were not fully *realized,* in the sense of reaching their current level of importance, until 1972. And it is the contention of this book that their importance has not been fully *realized,* in the sense of being understood and utilized, right up to the present day – over a hundred years since their inception and more than a century and a half since the two parties locked in at the top, with that one exception in 1912.

Nonetheless, for better or worse, the history of presidential politics on the left is predominantly a history of third party efforts. More often than not, one of the third party candidates was the only candidate saying what needed to be said. When Populist James Weaver, Socialists Eugene Debs and Norman Thomas, Progressives Robert La Follette and Henry Wallace, and the Green Ralph Nader ran for president their platforms were far closer to the spirit of this book than those of the Democrats or Republicans they ran against. The argument of this book is that a larger number of voters, usually limited to the dismal lack of vision exhibited by "mainstream" presidential candidates, will take modern day Debs's and La Follette's more seriously if they encounter them in the primaries. It is the argument that Sanders is testing.

Technically speaking, very few of us have actually ever voted for a candidate for president. Under the U.S. Electoral College system, that function is assigned to the "electors," the obscure figures for whom we actually do cast our votes on election day. Those electors pledged to the candidates who prevailed in the various states – which award them on a winner-take-all basis, with the exception of Nebraska and Maine which distribute some to the winners by congressional district, – actually cast the only votes that count when they convene on the

The Primary Route
Table 1: THIRD PARTY ELECTORAL VOTES

YEAR	PARTY	CANDIDATE	VOTE %	ELECTORAL VOTES	STATES WON
1832	Anti-Masonic	William Wirt	7.8	7	1
1836	Whig	Hugh White	9.7	26	2
	Whig	Daniel Webster	2.7	14	1
	Whig	Willie Mangum	0	11	1
	American/ Whig	Millard Fillmore	21.6	8	1
1860	*Northern Democratic (2nd)*	*Stephen Douglas*	*29.5*	12	1
	Southern Democratic	John Breckinridge	18.1	72	11
	Constitutional Union/Whig	John Bell	12.6	39	3
1892	Populist	James Weaver	8.5	22	5
1912	*Progressive (2nd)*	*Theodore Roosevelt*	*27.4*	*88*	*6*
	Republican	William Howard Taft	23.2	8	2
1924	Progressive	Robert La Follette	16.6	3	1
1948	States' Rights Democratic	Strom Thurmond	2.4	39	4
1968	American Independent	George Wallace	13.6	46	5

The Third Party Route

first Monday after the second Wednesday in December following the presidential election. So, technically speaking, the third party candidates named in Table I are the only ones who have ever received votes for the office of United States president.

Most people, however, do not have the technicalities of the Electoral College in mind when they're talking about presidential elections. Instead they're speaking of the "popular vote," which is usually their measure of how well a candidate did. Table 2 lists the strongest third party candidates by popular vote.

The U.S. is regularly referred to as having a "two-party" electoral system. The reality that the term describes can be seen in Table 2. Only eight candidates outside the top two parties of the day have exceeded 10% of the vote. The top two were former presidents who broke with their parties. Another two ran in the 1860 election that marked the transition when the Republicans permanently supplanted the Whigs in "top-two" party status. Since the Civil War, the only four third party candidates to record a double-digit vote were former President Theodore Roosevelt, who attempted to reenter the White House with a different political party and became the only candidate not a Democrat or Republican to finish in the top two over that period; Republican Senator Robert La Follette, who broke with his party to the left; former Democratic Governor George Wallace, who ran to the right; and H. Ross Perot, a billionaire who never held office but purchased advertising parity with the "major" parties out of his own pocket.

The picture in Table 1 is a bit messier, but essentially the same. In addition to the top popular vote getters, we find three 1836 Whig candidates who registered in the Electoral College because of their party's tactical decision to divide their vote among four candidates. Two more come from the 1860 election when the Democrats split into pro and anti-war factions and the last Whig would receive electoral votes, as his party handed over its "top two" party status to the Republicans. The only additional third party interlopers to legitimately break into electoral duopoly domination were the 1832 Anti-Masonics, arguably the first significant recognizable "third party;" the Populists, often treated as the paradigmatic American third party; and Strom Thurmond's States

The Primary Route

Rights campaign whose concentration in a few southern states allowed it to achieve Electoral College success out of proportion with its nationwide popular vote. (Perot, on the other hand, did not register in the electoral vote column because his much larger vote was so relatively evenly spread across the nation.)

Table 2: TOP THIRD PARTY FINISHES

YEAR	PARTY	CANDIDATE	VOTE %	ELECTORAL VOTES
1912	Progressive	Theodore Roosevelt[5]	27.4	88
1856	American/ Whig	Millard Fillmore	21.6	8
1992	Independent	H. Ross Perot	18.9	0
1860	Southern Democratic	John Breckenridge	18.1	72
1924	Progressive	Robert La Follette	16.6	13
1968	American Independent	George Wallace	13.6	46
1860	Constitutional Union/Whig	John Bell	12.6	39
1848	Free Soil	Martin Van Buren	10.1	0

The Third Party Route

The Socialists finished third a record seven times.

Table 3: THE THIRD PLACE FINISHERS
(and some notable fourths)

YEAR	PARTY	CANDIDATE	VOTE %	ELECTORAL VOTES
1832	Anti-Masonic	William Wirt	7.8	7
1836	Whig	Hugh Lawson White	9.7	26
	Whig	Daniel Webster	2.7	14
1840	Liberty	James Birney	0.3	
1844	Liberty	James Birney	2.3	
1848	Free Soil	Martin Van Buren	10.1	
1852	Free Soil	John P. Hale	4.9	

The Primary Route

YEAR	PARTY	CANDIDATE	VOTE %	ELECTORAL VOTES
1856	American/Whig	Millard Fillmore	21.6	8
1860	*Northern Democratic (2nd)*	*Steven A. Douglas*	*29.5*	*12*
	Southern Democratic	John C. Breckenridge	18.1	72
	Constitutional Union/Whig	John Bell	12.6	39
1864	None			
1868	None			
1872	Bourbon Democratic	Charles O'Conor	0.3	
1876	Greenback	Peter Cooper	1.0	
1880	Greenback	James Weaver	3.3	
1884	Greenback/Anti-Monopoly	Benjamin Butler	1.7	
1888	Prohibition	John St. John	1.5	
	Union Labor	Alson Streeter	1.3	
1892	People's (Populist)	James Weaver	8.5	22
	Prohibition	John Bidwell	2.2	
1896	National Democratic	John M. Palmer	1.0	
	Prohibition	Joshua Levering	0.9	
1900	Prohibition	John G. Woollen	1.5	
	Social Democratic	Eugene V. Debs	0.6	

The Third Party Route

YEAR	PARTY	CANDIDATE	VOTE %	ELECTORAL VOTES
1904	Socialist	Eugene V. Debs	3.0	
	Prohibition	Silas C. Swallow	1.9	
1908	Socialist	Eugene V. Debs	2.8	
	Prohibition	Eugene W. Chafin	1.7	
1912	*Progressive (2nd)*	*Theodore Roosevelt*	*27.4*	*88*
	Republican	William Taft	23.2	8
	Socialist	Eugene V. Debs	6.0	
	Prohibition	Eugene W. Chafin	1.4	
1916	Socialist	Alan Benson	3.2	
	Prohibition	Frank Hanly	1.2	
1920	Socialist	Eugene V. Debs	3.4	
	Farmer-Labor	Parley P. Christensen	1.0	
1924	Progressive	Robert La Follette	16.6	13
1928	Socialist	Norman Thomas	0.7	
1932	Socialist	Norman Thomas	2.2	
1936	Union	William Lemke	2.0	
1940	Socialist	Norman Thomas	0.2	

The Primary Route

YEAR	PARTY	CANDIDATE	VOTE %	ELECTORAL VOTES
1944	Texas Regulars		0.3	
	Socialist	Norman Thomas	0.2	
1948	States Rights Democratic	Strom Thurmond	2.4	39
	Progressive	Henry Wallace	2.4	
1952	Progressive	Vincent Hallinan	0.2	
1956	(Unpledged electors)		0.3	
	States' Rights	T. Coleman Andrews	0.2	
1960	Democratic	(Unpledged electors)	0.4	
	Socialist Labor	Eric Hass	0.1	
1964	Socialist Labor	Eric Hass	0.1	
1968	American Independent	George Wallace	13.6	46
1972	American Independent	John Schmitz	1.4	
1976	Independent	Eugene McCarthy	0.9	
1980	Independent	John Anderson	6.6	
	Libertarian	Ed Clark	1.1	
1984	Libertarian	David Bergland	0.3	
1988	Libertarian	Ron Paul	0.5	
1992	Independent	H. Ross Perot	18.9	
1996	Reform	H. Ross Perot	8.4	
2000	Green	Ralph Nader	2.7	

46

The Third Party Route

YEAR	PARTY	CANDIDATE	VOTE %	ELECTORAL VOTES
2004	Independent	Ralph Nader	0.4	
2008	Independent	Ralph Nader	0.6	
2012	Libertarian	Gary Johnson	1.0	

William Wirt, the longest serving Attorney General in U.S. history, was the first third party presidential candidate.

THE PARTIES

Anti-Masonic

The first third party campaign was run by William Wirt of the Anti-Masonic Party in 1832. Although the Federalist Party never elected another president after John Adams left office in 1801, they provided the only presidential level opposition to the Democratic-Republicans through the 1816 election. In 1820, President James Monroe got a free ride to reelection. In 1824 all competitors were Democratic-Republican. The 1828 election was contested by a Democrat and a National Republican. And in 1832, the Anti-Masonics made it a threesome.

This election cycle also introduced the phenomenon of the party nominating convention, the first of which was held by the Anti-Masonics when they chose Wirt, a former U.S. Attorney General, in September of 1831. The group had formed in New York State in reaction to the belief that a secret society – the Masons – held inordinate political influence and might have actually murdered one of its members who had threatened to publish a book revealing the group's secrets.

Wirt, who had once been a Mason himself, hoped to gain an endorsement at the Convention of the National Republican Party (not related to the current Republican Party), but that group went with Henry Clay and Wirt found himself with no real chance of election, winning less than 8% of the national vote and only the seven electoral votes of Vermont. The party elected governors in Vermont and Pennsylvania, as well as 25 members of Congress, but for the next presidential election, most of its members threw in with the National Republicans and other anti-Andrew Jackson forces to create the Whig Party.

Whig

Although Hugh Lawson White and Daniel Webster both appear in the charts of strong third party candidates, this is really a

The Third Party Route

technicality based on a strategy unique in the history of major party campaigns. The Whigs – whose name harkened back to a nickname attached to the original anti-British American revolutionaries, which in turned derived from anti-monarchical elements in the history of the United Kingdom – quickly became the principal opposition to the Democrats and contested the 1836 election with four separate candidates running in different parts of the country. Their main candidate was William Henry Harrison, later elected on a second try in 1840. When Harrison died a month into his term, he was succeeded by his running mate John Tyler, the first vice president to take the top office due to the death of a president. Tyler was not in fundamental agreement with party policy, however, and the Whigs actually expelled him from the party while he was in the White House. A remarkably similar scenario played out eight years later in 1848 when Whig candidate Zachary Taylor was elected president, died in office and was succeeded by a vice president, Millard Fillmore, who would be denied the party's nomination for president in 1852.

In 1856, the party did endorse Fillmore. That Fillmore had already been nominated by the American party reflected the fact that this new party had already largely supplanted the Whigs as the alternative to the Democrats. But by the time of the election, the newly-formed Republican Party surpassed them both and Fillmore finished third, although with the second strongest third place popular vote ever. The Whigs, surely the shakiest of the four parties ever to hold the American presidency, would never hold another convention, although 1860 Constitutional Union candidate John Bell is often described as being the Whig candidate as well. Former Whigs would eventually turn to the new Republican Party in large numbers.

Liberty

The Liberty Party was an anti-slavery party that twice ran James Birney, a former Kentucky legislator who was himself once a slave-owner. In 1840, the party was on the ballot in only nine of the 24 states where the general public voted (South Carolina's electoral votes were determined by its legislature), but Liberty's 0.3% showing was good enough for third place. In 1844, Birney made the ballot in 13 states and upped his vote to 2.3%. His vote was particularly significant in New York where it was three times that of the margin by which Democrat James Polk carried the state over Henry Clay, and with it the Electoral College – an outcome amenable to Birney who considered the Polk the less competent of the major party pro-slavery candidates. In 1848, the bulk of the party's support shifted to the Free Soil Party.

Free Soil

Former Democratic President Martin Van Buren, defeated in the 1844 election, wished to run again in 1848, but his position on slavery rendered him friendless at the Democratic convention, where he had failed at a renomination bid four years earlier. Turning to the Free Soil Party ("Free Soil, Free Speech, Free Labor and Free Men") Van Buren won the nomination of this party – organized to oppose slavery's expansion – over abolitionist Free Soil, and formerly Democratic, Senator John Hale of New Hampshire. Van Buren only appeared on the ballot of 17 out of 29 voting states (South Carolina would not hold a popular vote for presidential electors until after the Civil War), but his 10.1% of the vote still ranks as one of only eight double-digit results ever recorded outside the top two parties. Nationwide, he carried 30 counties and beat Democrat Lewis Cass in Massachusetts, New York and Vermont. He failed to win any electoral votes but was considered to have tipped the election to the Whigs, an outcome not distasteful to him.[6] The party also won 13 U.S. House seats, giving them the balance of power, a status they also held in 11 state legislatures.

Four years later, John Hale did become the party's candidate and also ran third, but with less than half the vote percentage of Van Buren's run, with the number of counties the party carried dropping to seven. The Free Soil Party, along with the Whigs, has generally been considered a seminal force in the creation of the Republican Party.

The Third Party Route

American

Denied the 1852 nomination of the Whig Party, which again chose a general – Winfield Scott – over a sitting president, Millard Fillmore four years later ran under the banner of the American Party. (The final convention of the Whig Party also unanimously endorsed his candidacy.) The American Party was a euro-nativist, anti-Catholic party, otherwise known as the "Know Nothings." The memorable nickname derived from the group's semi-secret origins and its members' profession that they "knew nothing" about any such organization. The party's detractors felt the nickname applied more broadly, however. At various points, the American Party elected five U.S. Senators, 50 House members (with one even serving as Speaker) and several governors.

But although only appearing on the ballot in 20 of the 31 popular balloting states, the new Republican Party immediately scored a second place finish – a status it has failed to match or better but once in over a century and a half since. Fillmore, seen as the centrist between pro and anti-slavery candidates, finished third with 21.6%.

Constitutional Union

By 1860, various floating Whigs and Know-Nothings backed the new Constitutional Union Party, an organization designed to waffle on the question of slavery and its expansion. The new party, which stood for "the constitution of the country, the union of the states, and the enforcement of the laws," nominated former Whig Senator, Speaker of the U.S. House, and Secretary of War, John Bell of Tennessee. When Steven Douglas could not win the necessary two-thirds of the Democratic nominating convention vote, southern Democrats nominated their own candidate, Vice President John Breckenridge of Kentucky.

Few voters today will realize that if no candidate wins an Electoral College majority the House of Representatives is then charged with picking a winner from the top three electoral vote getters. But John Quincy Adams had beaten Andrew Jackson to the White House in just that way following a four-way Electoral

The Primary Route

College split in 1825 and given the profound political splintering within the nation, a similar split seemed possible in 1860 as well. The Union Party's hope of winning the election rested on that kind of outcome.

Bell finished fourth overall with 12.6% of the vote, but the Democrats' split meant that he won the states of Virginia, Kentucky and Tennessee and finished third in the electoral vote, ahead of Douglas who had the second highest popular vote. Bell and Douglas actually ran a fusion slate of electors in New York. The party won two House seats.

This election brought to an end the most chaotic stretch of presidential politics in the country's history: From 1848-1860, two former presidents ran for reelection as candidates of a different party than the one they served in the White House, the Democrats split, and the Republicans replaced the Whigs as one of the governing parties. After the nation fought the Civil War that followed this election, a double-digit popular vote outside of the top two finishers would not occur again until 1912.

Greenback

Third party politics did not reemerge in any serious way on the presidential level until Peter Cooper's 1876 Greenback Party campaign – the first third party effort of what would prove to be the century-and-a-half-and-counting run of the Democrats and Republicans. In the prior three elections, the only non-Democrat-or-Republican candidate to amass a discernable number of votes was Charles O'Conor who drew a 0.3% scattering from 18 separate states (out of 37) in 1872, even though he had actually declined the nomination of the Straight-Out Democrats, a group that could not abide the mainstream Democrat endorsement of the Liberal Republican Party candidate, New York Tribune editor and one-time Whig Representative Horace Greeley.

The Greenbacks, initially a party of agricultural interests affiliated with the Grange, favored an inflationary policy of

Peter Cooper, inventor of Tom Thumb, the first American steam locomotive, was the first third party presidential candidate of the modern two-party era.

issuing paper money, known as "Greenbacks" – the practice during the Civil War – as opposed to the deflationary "hard-money" policy of the then-dominant Republicans. The question took on new urgency following the Panic of 1873, considered by many the first modern capitalist-era depression. The 85-year old Cooper, known for building the first American steam locomotive, had become a philanthropist whose name lives on today through New York City's Cooper Union college and Cooper-Hewitt National Design Museum. He made the ballot in 18 states, with 0.99% of the overall national vote. Republican Rutherford Hayes won, by a single electoral vote – despite being decisively defeated by the Democrat Samuel Tilden in the popular vote – but Cooper's vote total does not appear to have been a factor. From 1878 on, the party switched its name to Greenback Labor Party, symbolizing the start of a long tradition of farmer-labor politics. In 1880, it nominated James Weaver, a Greenback member of Congress from Iowa, for president. On the ballot in 34 of 38 states, drew 3.3% of the overall vote, winning six counties in four states. Twenty Greenback Party members served in the U.S. House.

Anti-Monopoly

In 1884, the Greenbacks endorsed Benjamin Butler. Butler, who had just finished a term as Democratic governor of Massachusetts and had previously run and lost a race for that office as a joint Democrat-Greenback candidate, was already nominated as the one-shot Anti-Monopoly Party's presidential candidate. Believing that there were Anti-Monopoly Democrats and Anti-Monopoly Republicans alike out there, at one point he hoped one of the major parties would actually nominate him. Butler proposed fusion slates with each of them in different states – the idea being to form a coalition with whichever happened to be the "lesser" party in a particular state. He succeeded in a couple. The arrangement was that if the combined vote on the two party lines constituted a plurality, the resulting electoral votes were to be distributed proportionally to the popular vote that the partner parties had received, but in most cases the potential partners proved reluctant. On the ballot in 30 states, Butler finished third with 1.7%, carrying two counties. Although this was the third third-place finish in a row for a Greenback-backed presidential candidate, the Greenbacks never fielded a national ticket again. Neither did the Anti-Monopoly Party, although it did manage to send one member to each branch of Congress.

The Third Party Route

Union Labor

In 1888, the short-lived Union Labor Party stepped into the slot filled by Greenback and Anti-Monopoly candidates in the prior three elections. Illinois Democratic state legislator and past Greenback gubernatorial candidate Alson Streeter made 24 state ballots, winning two counties and finishing fourth with 1.3% of the vote.

Prohibition

For longevity, no other third party can match the Prohibition Party which has fielded presidential and vice presidential candidates every four years since 1872. And the fact that its 2012 candidate won but 519 votes should not make us think that it was ever that way. The Prohibition Party may never have come close to winning a single electoral vote, but the fact is that in its day, prohibition was no isolated crank cause, but part of a broad reform movement. Prohibition did, after all, become the law of the land from 1919-1933.

The party's 1880 candidate, for instance, was Neal Dow, past Whig mayor of Portland, ME known as the "Napoleon of Temperance" and also an ardent abolitionist whose house was a stop on the Underground Railroad. Dow counted slavery's role in the West Indian rum production business as a factor in his prohibitionism. Prohibition Party presidential candidates recorded at least a 1% share of the vote in every election from 1884 through 1916, with the exception of 1896 when a multi-issue, split-off Prohibitionist candidacy held the mainline single-issue Prohibitionist candidate's vote to .9%. Former Republican Governor of Kansas John St. John appeared on 34 states' ballots in 1884 and drew a 1.5% vote. This was twice the number of ballots that Dow had appeared on and fifteen times as high a percentage of the vote as he had gotten. Many saw his 25,000+ New York votes, most presumed to have come from normally Republican-leaning voters, as a significant factor in Democrat Grover Cleveland winning the state – and with it the electoral vote majority – since Cleveland only carried New York by little

The Primary Route

Prohibitionist Party Mayor Susanna Salter of Argonia, Kansas, first woman elected mayor in the U.S.

over a thousand votes, even though he was then serving as its governor.

The Prohibitionists' vote share peaked at 2.2% in the 1888 and 1892 elections. The 1888 candidate, retired Brigadier General Clinton Fisk, made every ballot but South Carolina and gave the party one of its two third-place finishes, the other coming in 1900. Former Republican Representative John Bidwell of California made 35 state ballots in 1892, when there was wide anticipation of the party's presidential campaign merging with the People's Party, better remembered as the Populists. Running separately, the party did record its highest percentage ever, but this would only be good for a distant fourth behind the new party. They did maintain pockets of support, however: 1904 presidential candidate Silas Swallow ran first in eight counties across the nation, 1908 candidate Eugene Chafin won seven, and James Hanly won five in 1916.

The Third Party Route

In the eyes of many, the 1919 adoption of the Eighteenth Amendment establishing prohibition ended the need for the Prohibition Party. Its vote share fell under one percent in 1920 and declined by another two-thirds in 1924. And the passage of the Twenty-first Amendment repealing Prohibition in 1933 did not bring the party back – its 1936 vote was a mere 0.08%.   In its long history, the party has sent one member to Congress, Charles Randall of Los Angeles who won the 1914, 16 and 18 elections. Kittel Halvorson's election from Minnesota in 1890 is also cited as a Prohibition victory, but he was more widely known as a Populist. The Prohibitionist Party also has the distinction of electing the first female mayor in the country, Susanna Salter of Argonia, Kansas in 1887.

People's (Populist)

While the Prohibition Party has been the longest-running "third party," the Populists have surely been the most-studied. Following fifteen years of organizing by the National Farmers Alliance and Industrial Union, the People's – or Populist – Party constituted itself as a national political party in 1892. Its Omaha Platform supported government control of railroads and banks; expansive silver and greenback currency; a progressive income tax; direct election of U.S. Senators; and the initiative and referendum processes. Turning to 1880 Greenback candidate James Weaver to head its ticket, the party won more than ten percent of the nation's counties (276) and 8.5% of the overall vote. Coalitions with populist Democrat state organizations in agreement with the Omaha Platform resulted in Weaver winning Colorado, Kansas, Idaho, Nevada (where he took 66.7% of the vote under the rubric of the Silver Party) and North Dakota, states essentially uncontested by the Democrats.

The party elected over 40 members to the House of Representatives and another five to the Senate (where they were allied with an even larger bloc of Silver Senators). It was the first third party to command serious attention in what has turned out to

Populist James Weaver, one of very few candidates of the left to ever win electoral votes.

be a century-and-a-half span of Democratic/Republican two-party dominance. Not only would the Populists' breakthrough into the Electoral College be the first of only five times that a third party did so over the entire era, but it would also be the only time it was achieved by a candidate who had not previously held a prominent public office.

In 1896, however, the Populists endorsed U.S. Senator William Jennings Bryan, running as a Democrat on a free silver platform – albeit with a separate vice-presidential candidate of their own (who won 27 electoral college votes for the number two office) – a decision that would ever after be held up as the paradigm of how the American "two-party" system works by absorbing interests and groups that originate outside of it. For some observers this has represented the "genius" of the system, while for others it represents the system's original sin. Bryan lost to Republican William McKinley. The Populists nonetheless continued to field candidates in the next three presidential elections, even carrying five counties in Texas in 1900

Socialist

If the defining characteristic of an American third party is finishing third in a presidential contest, then the Socialist Party has been the country's quintessential third party, recording seven third-place finishes from 1904 to 1944. And the Socialists arguably rank with the Populists and the Prohibitionists as the big three of legitimate third parties, as opposed to vehicles for specific candidates, in the post-Civil War area. The Socialists generally advocated public ownership of the railroads and utilities, the eight-hour day, a minimum wage, a graduated income tax, unemployment and industrial accident insurance and abolition of the electoral college, while criticizing the other political parties as tools of the major financial interests.

Former American Railway Union leader and one-term Indiana Democratic state legislator Eugene Debs finished third in the presidential races of 1904, 1908, and 1920, although his highest percentage actually came when he finished fourth with 6% in 1912, a year when the party claimed more than a thousand local elected officials. He carried two counties; he had carried one four years earlier, and none in his prior two runs.

There had been talk of recruiting Debs as the Populist candidate in 1896 and he ran fourth on a hastily put-together Social Democratic ticket in 1900 before the Socialist Party came into

The Primary Route

place. In the Debs era, the party represented something of a home for "middle-of-the-road" Populists, i.e., "third-party" die-hards who hadn't agreed with backing Bryan. But while Debs's final 1920 candidacy – conducted from the Atlanta Federal Penitentiary, where he sat due to his opposition to the First World War – to some extent held the American left together, the creation of a largely non-electorally-oriented Communist Party markedly weakened the Socialist Party. In 1924, the Socialists opted to back Robert La Follette's Progressive candidacy instead of running one of their own.

When the Socialists returned to the presidential ballot with minister Norman Thomas as their candidate in 1928, he scored the first of his record four third place finishes (of six total races). But his 0.7% was the lowest total for any third place finisher since 1872. He tripled that in 1932, but would later finish third with percentages far lower than even that of 1928. The party ran presidential candidates through 1956 when they drew less than 0.1% of the vote. An offshoot Socialist Party USA has run presidential candidates since 1976, but they have usually achieved ballot access in fewer than ten states.

Progressive (1912) (Bull Moose)

In 1912, for the first time since the Republican Party's founding in 1856, when Whigs still walked the land, the party's candidate – William Taft, an incumbent president, no less – failed to finish at least second. Former Republican President Theodore Roosevelt attempted to deny Taft renomination and won nine of the twelve state primaries that were introduced to the process that year. (Wisconsin Senator Robert La Follette also won two.) Failing to convince a majority of the convention delegates, however, he opted for a third party run, opening the door for Woodrow Wilson, who won 40 states, to become the first Democrat elected president since 1892. Roosevelt carried six states and Taft just two. The party was popularly referred to as the Bull Moose Party, owing to the candidate's statement that, "I'm fit as a bull moose," after only a 50-page speech and an eye glass case that Roosevelt was carrying in his coat pocket prevented an attempted assassin's bullet from entering his lung.

The Third Party Route

Only twelve states produced outright majorities for any candidate in this race. The Socialist Debs beat Taft in three states and Roosevelt in two, and won 6% of the vote, making it the first – and only – time since 1860 that four candidates exceeded 5%. The Progressives elected members to the House in 1912 and 1914, but when Roosevelt endorsed Republican presidential nominee Charles Evans Hughes in 1916, the party rapidly faded away, with almost all Progressives returning to the Republicans. Unpledged Progressive electors did carry five counties in that race, however.

Farmer-Labor

The Farmer-Labor Party primarily existed in the state of Minnesota, where it sent members to the U.S. House and Senate in almost all of the elections from 1918 to 1942, after which it merged to become the Democratic Farmer-Labor Party. But in 1920 a national group by that name – growing mostly out of the post-World War upsurge in labor activity and much heavier on labor input than farmer – convened amidst some hope that things might be worked out for a Robert La Follette presidential candidacy. When that failed to happen they nominated Parley Christensen to run for the top office on a platform that advocated the eight-hour day, the right to collective bargaining, nationalization of railroads and utilities, repeal of the wartime Espionage and Sedition Acts and creation of a federal department of education. Only making it onto the ballot of 19 states, Christensen drew but 1% of the overall national vote, although he did get 19% in both Washington and South Dakota, trailing Democrat James Cox in the latter by fewer than 1,300 votes. Surely one of the most fascinating individuals ever to seek the presidency, over the course of his life Christensen held office in Utah and California, also ran in Illinois, and was likely the only presidential candidate to meet Vladimir Lenin. (He was impressed with the Soviet leader's command of English. Christensen himself spoke and taught the universal language Esperanto.) The national party became caught up in factional power struggles and fell by the wayside when an actual La Follette candidacy developed in 1924.

Robert La Follette, only non-Democrat ever endorsed for U.S. president by the AFL, with AFL president Samuel Gompers.

Progressive (1924)

Given that its unrelated 1912 namesake party was fundamentally a rebellion led by a former president, the Progressive Party of 1924 probably ranks as the most significant effort to move another party into the top two since the Populists.

The Third Party Route

Its ticket of Republican Senator Robert La Follette of Wisconsin and vice-presidential candidate Democratic Senator Burton Wheeler of Montana was the first, and still the only non-Democratic Party presidential ticket endorsed by the American Federation of Labor. Socialist Party members participated in the nominating convention. La Follette had voted against American entry into the World War and saw unions as a necessary counter to the increasing corporate concentration of wealth and power. The campaign supported reduced military spending, restricting monopolies, public power, nationalization of railroads and other industries, increased taxation of the wealthy, and the right to collective bargaining. "Battling Bob" La Follette beat the conservative Democratic candidate, former West Virginia congressman John Davis, in twelve states and won the electoral votes of his home state. He won 230 counties, 7.5% of the national total. Although La Follette died the next year, his sons, one of whom was elected to succeed him in the Senate, later revived the party as a significant factor on the state level. Its tradition also lives on in the continuous publication of the
Progressive Magazine, initially known as *La Follette's Weekly.*

Union

Until his assassination in 1935, there had been widespread anticipation that Democratic Senator Huey Long of Louisiana, leader of the Share Our Wealth movement, would run for the presidency in 1936. The largely forgotten Union Party candidacy of William Lemke is what actually emerged from the organizations that would have formed the base of a Long campaign that year. Like Long himself, the other leaders of these movements are also better remembered today than the actual presidential candidate of their one-shot political party. Sharing center stage were two quite right wing individuals, the Reverend Gerald L. K. Smith, who assumed the lead of the Share Our Wealth movement following Long's assassination, and Father Charles Coughlin of Michigan the preeminent radio evangelist of his day. Unlike most subsequent prominent radio evangelists, Coughlin was a Catholic, which lent the movement substantial ecumenical appeal – among Christians, that is. The third major figure, Francis Townsend, who led a national old-age pension movement, was a more reluctant political player.

Union Party presidential candidate, William Lemke.

Given the careers of the main personalities behind the Union Party it is understandably treated as a right wing phenomenon. By election day, the party's other principals had severed relations with Smith after he established his new organization, the Nationalist Front Against Communism and in the next of couple of years, Coughlin's publication, *Social Justice,* would go on to reprint a Josef Goebbels speech and defend the Third Reich's "social justice" policies. Townsend, on the other hand, did nothing more dramatic than support the 1944 presidential candidacy of Republican Wendell Wilkie.

Presidential candidate Lemke appears to have been cut from quite different cloth, however. An upper midwest Republican of the La Follette type, Lemke had been a central figure in the

The Third Party Route

North Dakota Nonpartisan League's 1916 campaign that won the state house on a platform of creating institutions like a state bank and state grain elevators that would free farmers from the control of outside interests. (The state-owned-and-operated Bank of North Dakota remains the only one of its kind in the country.) Although the League merged with the state Democratic Party in 1956, its origins were in the Republican Party and in 1936 Lemke was the state's nominally Republican Congressman. He had actually supported the election of Democrat Franklin Roosevelt in 1932 but broke with him over Roosevelt's unwillingness or inability to take actions such as blocking foreclosures that Lemke considered essential to help the struggling farmer.

Willing to make his bed with the strange fellows of the Union Party, Lemke ran on a platform that called for a living annual wage; a policy of "conscription of wealth as well as conscription of men" in time of war; federal conservation works creating "millions of jobs at the prevailing wages;" and upper limits on income and inheritance. While no one expected Lemke to win – throwing the election into the House of Representatives was about as optimistic an outcome as party backers might reasonably envision – the fact that the campaign had the backing of organizations with a combined membership running to the tens of millions did foster some high hopes at the outset. But the separate movements did not cohere and Lemke found himself running on the same ticket with candidates who appalled him, such as former Chicago mayor and current Union Party Illinois gubernatorial candidate, "Big Bill" Thompson, who denounced "Reds and Jewish bankers" during a campaign stop at the Chicago Nazi Clubs annual picnic.

Lemke only made the ballot in 34 states (New York and California not among them) and in eight of those it was under a party name other than the Union's. Roosevelt's 60.8% popular vote set the new record for a contested election, while Lemke fell a few votes short of 2% and exceeded the margin between Roosevelt and Landon only in New Hampshire, with his best showing of 12.8% coming in his home state. Nonetheless, Lemke joined President William Taft and Senator Robert La Follette as one of only three third party candidates to knock the

The Primary Route

Socialists out of a third place finish in the presidential race in the years from 1904-1944.

With the other principals losing interest after the unsuccessful campaign, Lemke soon found himself in control of the Union Party, but the organization did not even survive until the 1940 presidential campaign. Lemke continued his congressional career as a farm reform advocate until 1950. To the extent that this campaign is remembered at all it is usually treated as something of a *second-time-as-farce* revisiting of the Populists' third party experience.

Texas Regulars

Not an actual party, the Texas Regulars were a group of unpledged, conservative, dissatisfied-with-FDR electors who carried one county in Texas and 11.8% of that state's overall vote in 1944, which exceeded the 0.2% of the vote achieved by Socialist Norman Thomas in his final third place finish. The South's break with the Democrats on the presidential level starts here.

States' Rights Democratic

The product of a 1948 Democratic Convention walkout by southern delegates who objected to their party's endorsement of civil rights, the "Dixiecrats" hoped to deny the Democrats an Electoral College victory and ideally force the election into the House of Representatives where southern congressmen might extract states rights concessions from a possible winner.

South Carolina Senator Strom Thurmond appeared on the ballots of 17 states, drawing 2.4% of the overall vote. In most, he ran as the candidate of the States' Rights Democratic Party, finishing as high as second only in his home state, where he beat out Republican Tom Dewey with 20% of the vote. However, he took all 39 of the electoral votes from the only four southern states where he succeeded in being listed as the candidate of the official Democratic Party. These 39 votes were the highest total posted by a third party candidate since Teddy Roosevelt's 1912 run and were the highest total for a third place finisher in the Electoral College since the Whigs in 1860, when their candidate actually finished fourth in the popular vote. And he was the first third party candidate to carry more than a single county since Robert La Follette in 1924, winning 265 of them – 8.6% of the nation's total.

Progressive (1948)/American Labor

As the Dixiecrats had split with the Democrats from the right in 1948, the third twentieth century iteration of the Progressive Party did so from the left. Unrelated to its two previous namesakes, the new party ran Roosevelt's former Vice President Henry Wallace, who had also served as Secretary of Commerce in Harry Truman's cabinet until 1946. Wallace had broken with the administration largely over its increasingly antagonistic relations with the Soviet Union which only the prior year had been the country's principal ally in the war against the Axis powers. He and running mate Idaho Democratic Senator Glen Taylor were on the ballot in 45 states, ultimately finishing fourth with 2.4% of the vote – which made it the first election since 1920 with four candidates with 1% or more of the vote.

Although their overall vote nearly matched that of the Dixiecrats, the Progressives' support was spread over a much broader geographical area: where the Dixiecrats won 265 counties, the Progressive Party did carry not a single one. Expectations had been much higher early in the campaign, when it was thought that incumbent Harry Truman, who had succeeded to the presidency upon the death of Franklin Roosevelt, stood little chance of returning to the White House on his own initiative.

Since the Progressive candidates actually drew 44% of their entire national total running on the American Labor Party (ALP) ballot line in New York, that party arguably deserves near-equal billing, although it existed in but the one state, whose election laws permitted the type of "fusion" candidacies that allowed for aggregating votes gathered on more than one ballot line. The ALP had backed each of Roosevelt's reelection campaigns since 1936, but declined to back Truman. Given that the party's better-than 8% vote share far exceeded the less-than 1% margin by which Truman lost New York to Republican Tom Dewey, its role, and that of the Progressives, might have been the source of major recriminations had Truman not prevailed overall.

The Primary Route

The party also had endorsed Republicans, including Dewey in his successful 1937 run for New York City District Attorney.

The ALP was arguably a more successful party than the national Progressives, in that Vito Marcantonio, a former Republican Congressman, served six House terms as an ALPer (sometimes winning Democratic and Republican primaries as well) and another party member also served a partial term after winning a special election.[7]

A party that was not on the ballot also figured large in the fate of the Progressive party campaign. From 1924-1940, the head of the American Communist Party had stood as the party's presidential candidate, never drawing more than 0.3% of the vote. In the spirit of wartime unity, however, the Communists ran no candidate in 1944. But in 1948 they endorsed Wallace – who faced continual attack for being the recipient of that endorsement. A measure of just what a hot potato the Communists had become is the fact that when Republican hopefuls Tom Dewey and former Minnesota Governor Harold Stassen conducted what is considered to be the first radio debate between presidential candidates, the single topic at issue was whether the Communist Party should be outlawed, which the otherwise generally more liberal Stassen favored.

The Communists also endorsed the Progressives' second – and final – presidential candidate, San Francisco attorney Vincent Hallinan who finished third in 1952 with a vote percentage less than one-tenth of that recorded by Wallace when he finished fourth four years earlier. The Communists resumed running presidential candidates from 1968-1984, never exceeding 0.07% of the vote.

States' Rights

In 1956, the Dixiecrat banner was carried by T. Coleman Andrews, a former Commissioner of Internal Revenue who resigned the position because he actually opposed the federal income tax. Andrews won a couple of counties in Virginia, but his party had only a shadowy existence, being outpolled by Democratic unpledged electors who actually beat incumbent Republican President Dwight Eisenhower in South Carolina. Nationwide, the combination kept a total of 35 counties out of either the Republican or Democratic columns. The trend continued in 1960, when 71 counties in Louisiana and Mississippi cast pluralities for electors committed to neither the Democratic or Republican parties. In 1964, with Texan Lyndon Johnson on the ballot, the total was down to six, mostly in George Wallace's Alabama.

Socialist Labor

It took 18 tries before a candidate of the country's oldest socialist party would finish as high as third in a presidential election – in 1960, when the Socialist Party dad dropped from the field and Socialist Labor Party leader Eric Hass made the ballot in 15 states, and then again in 1964, when he appeared on 19 state ballots.

The party, founded in 1877 as the Workingmen's Party, arguably peaked in the 19th century, when it was composed largely of German immigrants and won elections in Chicago, St. Louis, Milwaukee and New Haven. It recorded its highest presidential election percentage – 0.29% – in 1900, but that was surpassed by the first candidacy of Eugene Debs who would subsequently run as the candidate of the Socialist Party which supplanted the SLP as the main institution of American socialism. Hass's 0.06% vote in 1960 was the lowest total recorded by a third place finisher since 1872. The party ran its last presidential candidate in 1976.

In both of Hass's third place finishes, his vote total was actually surpassed by the number cast for Democrats running as unpledged electors because they were unhappy with the national party candidate's stand on civil rights legislation. In 1960, such electors carried Mississippi, ran well in Louisiana and delivered a few more electoral votes to Virginia Senator Harry Byrd. In 1964 an unpledged Alabama group finished third nationwide.

American Independent

Disaffected southern Democrats constituted the third force in America for five of the six presidential elections since 1944. With the exception of Strom Thurmond in 1948, these voters were generally without a candidate, however. But in 1968 they found one in former Alabama Governor George Wallace whose 13.6%

The Primary Route

popular vote share was the highest third party candidate total since La Follette in 1924. His impact was arguably far greater than La Follette's, though. As had been the case with similar campaigns of the disaffected South, starting with the Dixiecrats in 1948, Wallace's vote was highly concentrated: he won 577 counties nationwide, not that many fewer than Democrat Hubert Humphrey's 693. This concentration won him 46 electoral votes from five states from the deep South (plus one "faithless" elector), the highest total ever for a third place electoral college finish.

Wallace recorded totals that were more than double that of the winning candidate's margin of victory in the 13 closest states and 17 overall. 13 of those states – and 185 electoral votes – went to Republican Richard Nixon, compared to four states and 73 electoral votes to Humphrey. The fact that Nixon's 112 electoral vote edge in these heavily Wallace-voting states exceeded his overall 110 electoral vote plurality seems a fair measure of Wallace's impact on the race.

Wallace's candidacy also ended a period when left-wing candidates finished third in presidential elections 12 or 13 – depending upon how the 1936 Lemke candidacy is viewed – out of 16 times from 1904-1964. An unambiguously left-wing candidate would not finish third again until Ralph Nader in 2000.

With Wallace reentering the Democratic Party in 1972 and running strong in its primaries until an attempted assassination ended his campaign, the American Independent Party became a far more typical third party when it nominated Republican Congressman (and John Birch Society member) John Schmitz of California that year. Schmitz was on 32 state ballots and received 1.4% of the vote. With the anti-war Senator George McGovern winning the ferociously contested Democratic nomination, five separate left-wing candidates mustered only a combined 0.35% of the vote.

Independents

In 1976, former Democratic Senator Eugene McCarthy of Minnesota, the man whose 1968 New Hampshire primary campaign began the unraveling of Lyndon Johnson's presidency, reached the final election ballot in 30 states and finished third with

The Third Party Route

a total under 1%. No longer identifiably a liberal or leftist, he became the first of a run of centrist independent candidates who would campaign under a hodgepodge of labels that varied from state to state.

Republican Congressman John Anderson of Ohio followed him with a much stronger 6.6% showing in 1980 after failing to win any of the Republican primaries he entered. Anderson was polling considerably higher at some points during the race and was included in the first League of Women Voters-organized presidential debate – which caused sitting President Jimmy Carter to boycott it. Anderson had ballot access in all 50 states and his support was so evenly spread that he didn't finish first in a single county in the entire nation. Ross Perot's first run in 1992 also came as an independent.

Libertarian

Percentagewise, the Libertarian Party's strongest showing came in its 1980 fourth-place finish – the only time its vote has exceeded 1%. The presidential candidate that year was California attorney Ed Clark. But it was the vice-presidential candidate, David Koch, who would go on to greater fame – along with brother Charles – for his prodigious funding of right wing candidates and causes. One of the richest men in the country, he contributed to his own 1980 campaign sufficiently that the ticket not only made it onto every state's ballot, but was able to run national television advertising, a quite unusual capacity for a third party.

The ticket supported abolishing Social Security, the Federal Reserve Board, welfare, minimum-wage laws, corporate taxes, agricultural price supports and subsidies and a host of Federal agencies. It also supported the abolition of restrictions on homosexuality and personal drug use. The party subsequently achieved third place finishes in 1984, 1988 and 2012. The 1988 candidate was Ron Paul – then in between stints as a Republican Congressman from Texas – who achieved greater notoriety with his 2008 and 2012 candidacies for the Republican presidential nomination. The party's 2012 nominee was Gary Johnson, former Republican governor of New Mexico. While never

The Primary Route

electing anyone to federal office, the Libertarians have won several state legislative seats.

Reform

The Reform Party formed around billionaire H. Ross Perot's second presidential run in 1996, but it was his first campaign in1992, conducted as an independent, that was by far the more remarkable. Perot took 18.9% of the vote that year, the highest third party total since former President Theodore Roosevelt in 1912. It was also the highest percentage ever achieved without carrying a single state and therefore not winning a single electoral vote. And you'd probably also have to go back to the Roosevelt Bull Moose campaign to find as widespread a sense that a third party candidate might actually be able to pull it off. Perot led both Bush and Clinton in polls at one point, on the strength of which the Commission on Presidential Debates included him in the first three-way debates. And most respondents told pollsters they considered him to have won the first of them.

Perot, a self-made businessman who had never run for or held public office before, did not easily take to the political process, however, going so far as to withdraw from the race for 2 ½ months during the middle of the campaign. His running mate, retired Vice Admiral and seven-and-half-year Vietnam War POW, James B. Stockdale, largely chosen to meet the requirement of several states that a presidential candidate have a running mate, was never truly an engaged candidate. But unlike any previous candidate of the electronic media era, Perot faced no problem matching the media buys of the Republicans and Democrats, buying 30 and 60 minute "infomercials" on all three of the major television networks of the day. He won 16 counties in seven states and remains the only third party candidate to win even a single county since George Wallace in 1968. He finished second overall in Maine and Utah. Many Republicans credited his candidacy with defeating Bush, but an exit poll showed his supporters split down the middle as to which of the other two they would have chosen had Perot not been on the ballot.

The Debate Commission, controlled by the two major parties since 1988, changed its rules so as to disallow Perot's

The Third Party Route

participation in 1996. And while he again fared well compared to the norm for third party candidates, with the fifth highest percentage of the 20th century – his vote count was still less than half his 1992 total and he didn't finish first in any county. Based on the 1996 race, the party qualified for matching funds in 2000, when past and future Republican Pat Buchanan received its nomination. He did not draw votes at anything like the rate Perot had, however, and the party lost access to federal funding. By 2004, when the Reform Party backed Ralph Nader, the party's nomination only gained him ballot access in seven states. The party has continued to exist and nominate candidates in 2008 and 2012 but the national vote totals have been limited to three digits.

The Reform Party, which has envisioned itself as a third party of the center has generally supported a balanced federal budget, limits on campaign contributions and the outlawing of political action committees, and opposition to free trade agreements. Its greatest success was the 1998 election of former professional wrestler Jesse "The Body" Ventura as governor of Minnesota.

Green

The Green Party is best known for consumer advocate Ralph Nader's 2000 presidential campaign that netted 2.7% of the national vote, although Nader was only on the ballot in 43 states plus the District of Columbia, a total lower than that available to both the Reform and Libertarian candidates. The campaign's issues included universal healthcare, tax reform favoring the middle and working class over corporations, increasing the minimum wage and labor rights, dramatic escalation of environmental protections, reform of the nation's drug policies and the pervasiveness of corporate influence.

As the closeness of the Bush-Gore race became clear with the approach of election day, Gore began to appeal directly to Nader voters while a group called the Republican Leadership Council ran pro-Nader/anti-Gore television ads in three states. Although the Republicans' one-sided message was not what the Greens themselves would have put on the airwaves, they never had the funds to run their own pro-Nader ads. With Nader stressing the

The Primary Route

Ralph Nader – most recent third place finisher from the left.

goal of a 5% nationwide vote that would secure federal funding for the Greens in the next presidential election, some supporters established websites on which would-be Gore and Nader voters from different states might pledge to vote for each other's candidate, giving Gore a vote in a close state in exchange for a Nader vote in a state that was not close but would still count toward his national total. The Democrat-controlled Justice Department ordered the websites shut down, however – a move subsequently ruled illegal by a federal court.

With Bush elected as a result of a hotly contested 537-vote margin in Florida, many Democrats blamed Nader and the Greens for Bush's victory, as he had drawn 97,488 votes in the state. While some polls support that conclusion, Al From, chair of the centrist Democratic Leadership Council with which Gore was affiliated, argued that "The assertion that Nader's marginal vote hurt Gore is not borne out by polling data. When exit pollers asked voters how they would have voted in a two-way race, Bush actually won by a point. That was better than he did with Nader in the race." What seems clear is that while the Nader vote *was only one of many factors* that *might* have moved the state to the Bush column – in a race so close that the candidates of seven other parties besides the Greens also recorded vote totals greater than Bush's margin of victory – *it was one of the factors.*[8]

Whatever the truth may be in the matter, significant numbers of both Green Party activists and potential Green Party voters have shied away from Green Party presidential politics in subsequent years. Nader would also finish third in the next two elections, but not as the Green candidate. The Greens' 2004 candidate David Cobb emphasized campaigning only in "non-battleground" states in the race between Bush and John Kerry and some of his supporters actively encouraged a Kerry vote in those states. His vote was less than one-tenth that of Nader's.

The Greens have never elected a congressional representative, but they have elected a handful of state legislators and enjoyed considerable success in a variety of local government arenas in more than twenty states, including electing a mayor in Richmond, CA and majority stakes in a number of town councils.

Conclusion

The Democratic and Republican Parties won't last forever; nothing does. But some things do last for a long time. Will the Democrats and Republicans be around, say, in 500 years? Probably not. Will they still dominate in 50 years? Well, the history of the country's third party presidential campaigns suggests that might not be such a bad bet. After all, some historians call the Democrats the oldest political party in the world and the junior party here, the Republicans, has failed to finish in the top two in a presidential race only once since arriving on the scene in 1856, and then only when one of their own former presidents jumped ship and ran against their current nominee.

The third party challenges keep coming, but since 1924 only twice have candidates outside of the Republican or Democratic parties gotten even ten percent of the popular vote and only two of them have won any electoral votes. On the evidence, it seems difficult to make much of a case that a third party is likely to supplant one of the frontrunners any time soon.

But while new third parties have pretty well been frozen out of the top presidential slots for the past century and a half,

The Primary Route

another route to the top has existed now for most of that time, in the form of the presidential primaries within the major parties. And yet, even as those primaries have steadily grown in significance, there has never been a systematic attempt from the American left to utilize the primary process consistently to put its case before a national electorate.

The primaries, of course, have traditionally been treated as a transitory, one-shot, candidate-oriented process – the Bernie Sanders campaign being the latest instance – so the objective difficulties of actually bending them to a long-running purpose would not be insubstantial. But it's the subjective factor that has rendered those very real objective difficulties moot: a broad consensus on the value of undertaking such an effort has simply never emerged. The non-consensus that does prevail has multiple causes, certainly, but one of the most enduring, or at least one of the most frequently articulated, is the strain of left opinion that objects to doing anything within the existing major parties. More precisely, it's the view that objects to working within the Democratic Party, since it has been quite some time since anyone on the left has seriously proposed doing anything with the Republican Party.

Red-Green-Red in Germany

Garrison Keillor once remarked that "If you watch television news, you will know less about the world than if you just drink gin straight out of the bottle." Harsh, but fair, and particularly so when it comes to learning about the world outside the U.S. No, what political scientists call "comparative government" is just not all that big a thing in American news programing. Or in plain English, we don't generally tend to hear a whole heck of a lot about how government works in any other country.

Clearly, our lack of knowledge of any other political system to compare it with only diminishes our ability to understand our own. So we can't be too surprised when Americans may express a desire to emulate the success of third parties in other countries, without always understanding the specific way that such a party may function in those countries, in comparison to how one can function here in the U.S.

The fourth chapter of this book characterized our presidential election as a "subtractive" process, meaning that since our system only requires pluralities to win, we may run up against a situation where voting for the candidate from a third party that we *really* prefer – rather than for the Democrat that maybe we aren't so hot on, *but definitely prefer* to the alternative – might inadvertently help elect the one we *really didn't want* – probably a Republican. In other words, casting our preferred vote might *subtract* from the chances for the better of the two realistic possibilities.

This aspect of the system most recently came to the fore over the question, also alluded to in the first chapter, of whether a percentage of Ralph Nader's 2000 Florida or New Hampshire vote

The Primary Route

could be thought of as somehow having been "subtracted" from Al Gore's potential vote – in the sense that a plurality of Nader's voters would have gone for Gore were there no Nader option on the ballot. And there was the further question of whether that difference would have been sufficient to elect George W. Bush.

The argument was also made that, in contrast to the actual November election, the presidential primary (and caucus) process leading up to the nominating convention was an "additive" one, in the sense that a vote for the presidential candidate you *really* wanted to see get the nomination might later in a sense be *added* to those cast for other candidates, candidates who, while obviously not your first choice, were still more to your liking than some others. And to the degree that this was the case, it did away with the risk of unintentionally helping the candidate you loved the least. The crucial difference here stemmed from the fact that you were casting ballots for delegates to a nominating convention where a simple plurality did not settle the question. In theory, if no candidate had majority support, your candidate's delegates might line up with the other most like-minded delegates behind the most like-minded candidate who emerged in a position to win the nomination. This would be an "additive" process.

The difference in the nature of these stages of the presidential election process is fundamental. No matter what we might think of it, no matter whether we like it or not, this difference means that it is principally in the primary process, rather than the November election, that we have our first best opportunity to get behind candidates running the race that needs to be run and saying the things that need to be said, even if they may not yet have the wherewithal to win. And to the extent that this central proposition of this book is true, it means that so far as our opportunities for carrying an egalitarian, anti-militarist perspective into the American national debate are concerned, the presidential primaries are a *sine qua non* element. If we can't figure out how to deal with them, we'll never really be a part of the big show.

The most common example of an "additive" process, in the sense that it's used here, is what's generally called a parliamentary system – where separate parties can add their votes to form a majority that will jointly name the head of the government. The

Red-Green-Red In Germany

current system in Germany – where every government since World War II, first in the West and then in the unified country, has formed from a coalition of parties – is virtually a textbook example of that type of parliamentary system. As such, Germany provides a distinct contrast to the way we choose our presidents here in the U.S. At the same time, while the German political structures may be quite different from ours, we political activists in the U.S. can easily recognize and perhaps identify with many of the major currents of the left that have coursed through German politics: An ongoing challenge to permanent militarization which encompassed a vehement anti-Vietnam War movement, a new wave of feminism that profoundly changed society, and an ecology movement that has sought to fundamentally reorder the economic system that is driving our current ecological degradation. All have all left their marks on the country's current political landscape.

The activists of the German "new left" in the above-mentioned movements have enjoyed a substantially greater presence in their political system than their American counterparts. And as is the case in the U.S., it's been many years since Germany's new left was new: "new" refers to what was new in the 1960s. Many of these new leftists – although not all – have utilized a third party route to increase their impact. That is to say, they utilized a new third party; there have always been at least three parties represented in the parliament of West Germany and later the unified Germany. And given that most other countries also have more than two significant parties, it's perhaps only to be expected that there are those in the U.S. who argue not only that third parties are the route to relevance for the American left as well, but that it is precisely its failure to break out of the confines of the Democratic Party and instead create a new party that has kept America's left from achieving similar success.

The following brief tour through the recent history of the German left is designed to highlight the fundamental differences between the American presidential election process and the method of choosing a head of government, or chancellor, in the German parliamentary process; to distinguish the differing roles of third parties in the two systems; and to compare and contrast the "additive" German parliamentary system, the "additive" American presidential nominating process, and the "subtractive" American presidential election process.

The German New Left

Pre-World War II Germany's "old left" parties – primarily the Social Democrats and Communists – were immensely more significant than any of their American counterparts have ever been. In the post-war partition of the country, the successor to the pre-war Communist Party operated an essentially one-party state in East Germany – the former Soviet postwar occupation zone properly known as the German Democratic Republic. In the Federal Republic of Germany, or "West Germany" – the former American, British and French zones – the Social Democratic Party (SPD) became the first opposition party, i.e., the second largest party. In the East, the SPD was required to merge with the Communists into the governing Socialist Unity Party, a move denounced by the SPD of the West. The Communists would eventually be outlawed for a time in the Federal Republic.

Meaningful debate in the East was generally consigned at best to the fringes of society as the forcibly merged single party took on the repressive, undemocratic characteristics that much of the world would ever after associate with official Communism. Free political discussion would not reappear publicly in a major way until after Mikhail Gorbachev's ascension to power in the Soviet Union.

In West Germany, many German new leftists opted to wipe the political history slate clean and instead immerse themselves in "extra parliamentary" activity under the aegis of no political party at all – a trend in tune with a broader, nebulous new left also sprouting up in the United States and throughout western Europe during the 1960s. The early rumblings of all of the new lefts in the various nations included dissatisfaction with governments' now-permanent war footing and, in particular, the nuclear arms race. In Germany, the trigger for many who turned over from "old" to "new" left was the Social Democrats' break with neutralism as the party acquiesced to West Germany's lining itself up with the West in the Cold War.

Red-Green-Red In Germany

The SPD

The SPD (Sozialdemokratische Partei Deutschlands) is the oldest socialist party in the world, with roots in parties that date back to 1863. It has prevailed as the principal factor of the German left through the country's defeat in World War I, the Nazi era, the devastation of World War II, and the Cold War Era division into two countries. Its first political program, formulated in the town of Gotha, was famously critiqued by Karl Marx himself. His criticisms were taken to heart and leaders in tune with his ideas oversaw the party's rise to become the largest group in the German Parliament by the eve of the First World War.

Much of the international socialist movement of the prewar era was firmly antiwar, arguing that the worker of one country had no business fighting the worker of another. Nevertheless, when World War I broke out, most of the socialist parties ultimately followed their nation's flags into battle. When the SPD parliamentary delegation supported Germany's entrance into the war – nearly unanimously – an antiwar Independent Social Democratic Party quickly split off. And after the war had triggered Russia's Bolshevik Revolution, there came a German Communist Party as well. The Independents eventually rejoined the SPD, but the inability/unwillingness of the Communists and the SPD to negotiate some type of working unity in the post-World War I years is generally considered a substantial factor in Adolf Hitler's rise to power.

The SPD reemerged as the prime party of the West German left following the Nazi years and the Second World War, but West Germany's first parliaments were dominated by the conservative Christian Democratic Union (CDU). The CDU and its Bavarian affiliate, the Christian Social Union, governed in coalition with the Free Democratic Party (FDP), which became Germany's perennial third party for many years. Generally considered a "liberal" party, not in the American sense of "left, but not too left," but rather in a distinctly European sense of "liberal," the FDP might be called libertarian in the U.S.

In 1966, the SPD entered its first government since 1930, replacing the FDP as the junior partner in a so-called "grand coalition," with its principal opponents in the CDU. This coalition agreement was itself something of a prod to the further

The Primary Route

development of the new left, as it involved the SPD dropping its previous opposition to the Emergency Laws legislation that granted the government increased police and surveillance powers and was greatly reviled by much of the extra parliamentary left. The country's 1968 street protests against that legislation, the Vietnam War, and neo-nazism, were sufficiently memorable that many dissidents of the day would be known as "68ers" ever-after.[9]

In 1969 the SPD became the senior party in a coalition government with the FDP and named its first post-World War II chancellor. In 1972 it finished first in a German election for the first, and thus far only, time since 1930. All told, the SPD held a share of government power for 16 consecutive years, until 1982.

The Greens

A workers party for as long as there have been workers parties, the SPD remained a relentless critic of the distribution of wealth and power in the country's economic system. It was not, however, particularly critical of industrialism itself. So while many in the developing new left might have seen a relationship with the SPD, or perhaps at least its youth group, as inevitable, for others the SPD's failure to take on the negative environmental impact of the capitalist economy constituted a permanent bar to involvement, with the party's embrace of nuclear power being particularly problematic. Hence the development of the Greens.

The German Greens were neither the first party to campaign on a predominantly environmental platform, nor the first to be called "Green," but they were the first such party to rise to national prominence. After a respectable first showing by a loosely organized group in the 1979 European Parliament elections, the Greens formally constituted themselves as a party the following year, proclaiming the "Four Pillars of the Green Party" to be social justice, ecological wisdom, grassroots democracy and nonviolence. SPD Chancellor Helmut Schmidt dismissed them as "environmental idiots who will have disappeared again soon."

Although never a party fully of the German left tradition, in that they contained strains of traditional environmentalist

Red-Green-Red In Germany

German 68ers like future Defense Minister Joschka Fischer, left with megaphone, worked their way into the system.

thinking that held no fundamental disagreement with the capitalist system, the Greens would be the prime conduit to the mainstream for several strands of activism then bubbling up from within the extra parliamentary left in addition to environmentalism. Advocating gender equity at a level not before experienced in the country's political scene, the Greens decreed that 50 per cent of party positions would be occupied by women. To realize this goal, the party adopted the use of the 'zipper' principle – alternating men's and women's names on its electoral lists.[10] By 1982 the Greens passed the five percent threshold required for party representation in a couple of German state parliaments and in 1983 did so on the federal level.[11]

The early Greens tended to two political camps: *Fundis* and *Realos* – the fundamentalists and the realists. Among other things, the Fundis held that when a conflict arose between a parliamentary deputy's personal view and a position that had been voted on at a party conference, the party's position must prevail, a stance arguably at odds with that of the German constitution. In the party's early years, the Greens actually rotated their parliamentarians – requiring them to leave office

*The German Greens distinguished themselves for prominent female leaders
like party co-founder Petra Kelly.*

halfway through their terms to be replaced by the next Green
candidate on the election list.

But while the practice of mandated gender equity proved
to be a keeper, for the most part it was the Realos who prevailed in
the intra-party struggle and eventually opened the way for a series
of Red-Green coalition governments on the state level starting in
1985 and finally, in 1998, in the federal government. With only
6.7% of the vote, the Greens were much the junior partner in that
government – as SPD Chancellor Gerhard Schröder put it, "In a
red-green coalition it has got to be clear: The bigger one is the cook,
the smaller one is the waiter." But they *were* in government, the
first new party to participate in a West German government since
the Social Democrats themselves, who had been in government
before in pre-Nazi Germany. The Greens have by now formed part
of governing coalitions in 13 of 16 German states and have been
the top party in one of them.

Red-Green-Red In Germany

The Greens can certainly take some pride of achievement regarding at least two of the party's "four pillars." In the "social justice" area they undoubtedly deserve some of the credit for feminism's spread throughout German society and the party's push for "ecological wisdom" figured substantially in the country's adoption of a plan to phase out nuclear power. Whether they've had any lasting impact regarding "grassroots democracy" is less clear. And as for "nonviolence," it was arguably the participation of the Greens, in particular that of their former 68er Foreign Minister, Joschka Fischer, that proved instrumental in legitimizing the country's first military engagement since the Second World War when the Red-Green government decided to back the 1999 NATO bombing of Serbia during the Kosovo War.

Another Shade of Red

By her third term as Chancellor, Angela Merkel of the Christian Democrats had become arguably Europe's best known and most influential political leader. Ironically, however, in two of the three elections from which she emerged as chancellor, the parties of the German left had the votes in parliament to block her rise to power and instead form a government of their own, yet opted not to do so.

In these elections, the SPD and the Greens had been joined on the national scene by a third party of the left which was called just that – the Left Party. But while three of the 16 German states have been governed by SPD/Left coalitions – including one SPD/Left/Green coalition and one in which the Left was the lead party – these have all been in the former East Germany. On the national level, the SPD and Greens have thus far ruled out a coalition with the Left Party. As a result, in 2005 and in 2013, rather than trying to become the lead party of a three-party coalition of the left, the SPD again opted in favor of a "grand coalition" in which it served as junior party to the CDU.

The Greens and, especially, the SPD have three principal objections to the Left Party's participation in a federal coalition government: the party's East German origins, Oskar Lafontaine, and NATO.

The Primary Route

The Left Party's East German Origins

Most of the Left Party's support lies in the states that comprised the former East Germany, where it draws votes on a level similar to that of the SPD and the CDU: In 2013 it polled 23 % in the East and only 6% in the former West Germany. The source of this eastern support, however, also constitutes the party's most significant stumbling block: It is the successor to the Socialist Unity Party that governed the German Democratic Republic.

After the series of events culminating in the opening of the Berlin Wall in 1989, the Socialist Unity Party rapidly changed its leadership, its name, and even its membership: longtime East German Premier Walter Ulbricht and associates quickly exited office, it became the Party of Democratic Socialism (PDS) in 1990, and it quickly lost an estimated 95% of its 2.3 million members. Still, it received 16% of the vote of the East that year and has maintained a solid core of support there ever since. But if the PDS wasn't what its predecessor had been in the East, it really amounted to hardly anything at all in the West, where it would poll only about 1% up until 2005.   Far and away the most controversial of the German parties represented in Parliament, the Left Party continually confronts the question of whether it is in some way responsible for what happened in the East Germany of the past and the further question of just how bad the East German government actually was. In 2001, for example, the head of the PDS officially acknowledged the injustice of building the Berlin wall in 1961, but asserted that the PDS was not to blame, as it had not even existed at that time.

Oskar Lafontaine

Shortly after the Red-Green Coalition took power in 1998, its unity was shattered in spectacular fashion. The major problems didn't arise between the coalition's partners, though, but within the SPD itself, as the party's chairman and government Finance Minister, Oskar Lafontaine, abruptly resigned both positions due to his objection to German participation in the NATO bombing campaign in the Kosovo War – as well as to what he considered to be the party's general drift to the right in economic policy.

Lafontaine subsequently reemerged in the public eye as

Red-Green-Red In Germany

part of a group of dissidents to the left of the SPD that ran a coordinated campaign with the PDS in 2005 and in 2007 merged with it to form the Left Party. Although there is understandably no official policy in this regard, there remain those in the SPD who will probably never welcome a coalition with a party in which their former chairman who deserted them plays any role. You might say Lafontaine is the twenty-first century German Teddy Roosevelt who never came home.

NATO

While the Red-Green coalition opposed America's 2003 invasion of Iraq, it did support the Afghanistan War and send troops. The Left Party did not support either of these wars and in some sense picked up the torch for the antiwar sentiments that dominated the German left from the end of the Second World War until the Kosovo War. The party also supports Germany's withdrawal from NATO, which many, even on the left, argue places it beyond the pale of the country's pro-West consensus. In the long run, it will undoubtedly be questions of current party policy such as this – as opposed to historical matters – that will be decisive in determining the course of German left unity.

Resistance to any future grand coalition of the German left goes both ways. Lafontaine argues that the Left Party needs to "always make very clear that we do not belong to the neoliberal party cartel."

France

Before we leave Europe, perhaps to sharpen the eye maybe a bit more to the ways that political systems can vary in their particulars, let's look at France, which has a parliamentary system that chooses a prime minister in a fashion similar to Germany's, but utilizes a different electoral process to get there. One distinctive difference of the French system is that it potentially, and usually, involves two rounds. The system is designed to allow the voters to "vote their hearts" in the first round, as people split their votes among such a large number of parties that fewer than 10% of the districts may actually produce a majority vote winner in that round. In contrast, in the second round run-offs between the top two finishers from the first round, most voters will find themselves

The Primary Route

having to "vote their heads," settling for finalists who might have been their second, or even worse, choice in the prior round – or perhaps just voting for the one they dislike least. In any case the role for what we in American think of as "third parties," or parties outside the "top two," is fairly open. You give it your best shot in the first round and you take the best available option in the second round.

But just to remind us that there is probably no such thing as a perfect, foolproof system, there was the case of the 2002 French presidential election. Yes, the French elect a president as well as a prime minister. If you are unclear on how this works, don't be too concerned – it's unclear how clear the French themselves are on it. When French voters cast their first ballot, "from-the-heart" votes that year, they spread them far more broadly than usual. Six parties of the left drew from one to six percent of the vote: Workers' Struggle, the Citizens' Movement, the Greens, the Revolutionary Communist League, the French Communist Party and the Radical Party of the Left. The result was that the Socialist Party candidate received only 16.2%, finishing behind Jean-Marie Le Pen of the right wing, anti-immigrant National Front, and failed to make the runoff.

While the idea of a socialist party not finishing in the top two may seem normal enough in the U.S., that's not the case in France, where Socialist Francois Mitterand, who served two terms from 1981-1995, has arguably been the country's most influential president since Charles DeGaulle. This would, in fact, be one of only two times that a socialist presidential candidate failed to make the second round since the country reinstated direct presidential elections in 1969 (and the Socialists indeed came back and won the presidency again in 2012).

The 2002 French presidential final election then provided an example of a nation voting for the candidate it disliked the least in numbers not likely to be equaled any time soon. While incumbent Jacques Chirac's vote rose from 19.9% in the first round to 82.2% in the final, Le Pen's vote only went from 16.9% to 17.8%. This 60.3% increase from the first to second round compared to LePen's mere 0.9% meant that the sitting president had won the votes of nearly 99% of those who had voted for someone other than the top two finishers in the first round. Still, the election was something of a national embarrassment for France – and for none more than the French left that had spread its support widely but not well in the first round.

The United Kingdom

And before heading home let's make one last stop in the United Kingdom, where we find a political system that's something part-way between the German system and our own. As in Germany, in the U.K. a parliamentary majority chooses the head of government, the prime minister. But unlike Germany with its separate party votes, or France with its two-stage elections, the U.K. has a simple "first past the post" system, where it takes only a simple plurality to win a seat, the same "subtractive" set-up as in our presidential election and most of our congressional elections. This means that with three major parties – Conservatives, Labor and Liberal Democrats – U.K. voters often faced the same dilemma that would-be third party voters encounter in American elections – that is, a vote for the candidate they actually want the most could increase the chances of a victory for the candidate they want the least. And unlike Germany, single party governments are the norm in the United Kingdom.

Traditionally, many voters of the center/left – Labor and Liberal Democrats – dealt with this situation by voting "tactically," choosing whichever of the two parties' candidates appeared to have the better shot of beating the Conservative. The practice has presumably been iced for the foreseeable future, however, by the Liberal Democrats' 2010 decision to enter into a now-dissolved Conservative-led coalition government. For now, the Labor Party stands on its own on the left on the national level, as the Liberals have been supplanted by the Scottish National Party, but the U.K. history of tactical voting nonetheless remains a notable example of voters adapting to a less than ideal political structure.

The "take away" from our European journey? Although they go under a variety of names: social democrats, greens, leftists, socialists, or laborites, the activists on the left of the various countries probably don't differ from us on the American left that much in their overall goals or viewpoints. Most appear to think their governments should spend less on the military and more on the poor. They think that workers deserve greater rights and wages and that corporations should have their power and profits checked. The way they operate politically, on the other hand, varies immensely from country to country. An electoral approach quite to the point in one country may be totally irrelevant or even counterproductive in another.

Are the German, French, and British lefts in any way superior to the American left? In the final analysis it's not clear what such a question might actually mean. Certainly we on the hazy American left can only envy the degree to which these movements have consistently brought their case for democratizing the direction of their economies and developing an anti-militarist foreign policy before a far wider audience then we generally manage to do. On the other hand, the inability of the European left to pull together at important moments has brought some dire consequences, and principles have not always withstood the pressures of the moment.

But if there is one way in which we might conclude that the European left have the advantage over their less well defined American counterparts, it is in the degree to which they have mastered the specifics of their own political systems. Hopefully the fact that third parties on the left play a significant role in two of the countries we've just looked at will not actually serve to further confuse the situation rather than to clarify it. For the entire point of our European junket is to show that these parties are successful because of specific aspects of their systems that don't have a parallel in the American presidential final election – but do have similarities with our presidential nominating process.

The reason that our presidential campaign debate so dominates American politics is the simple fact that the outcome of a presidential election is, by a large margin, the most important element in determining our national policy. Unlike these three European nations, we do not form our governments in our legislative body – Congress. And while recent Congresses have established a reputation for obstructionism, and very successful obstructionism, at times, the fact is that it's the executive rather than the legislative branch that determines the lion's share of the day-to-day functioning of American government. Even the Supreme Court – which may limit the power of a president – is ultimately chosen by a president.

Among the many effects of this difference is that the U.S. has tended tend to have more "big tent" parties, parties that may encompass a much wider range of political views than would be the norm in many other countries. The recent ideological tightening-up among Congressional Republicans notwithstanding, American political parties very rarely operate under any kind of political discipline, with the exception of procedural votes such as the election of legislative leadership. Where European parties will present a common program that represents their goals for governing if elected, the fact is that in the U.S. governing principles are primarily established in the White House rather than on Capitol Hill. So when an American legislator may vote "off" from general party policy it is generally not nearly as serious a matter as it might be for a European legislator to do so. It is not clear that American third party advocates have always appreciated this difference.

While it is true that American third parties have experienced smatterings of success in recent years on the local or even state level, the structure of the presidential election process has kept them largely stymied on that level for a century and a half now. The German Greens might throw themselves into the national election and eventually emerge with enough votes and seats in parliament to form a government with the SPD, which some of the party base may have considered the "lesser of two evils" in comparison to the Christian Democrats. The SPD could likewise recognize that for all that they might not love about the Greens, the party still had a lot more in common with them than with the Christian Democrats. A process like this is never without its hard feelings, yet the German left moved on, with subsequent substantial success. And the Left Party is now added to the mix.

But a comparable opportunity does not exist for American Green Party presidential candidates, for example, or for the candidates of any other third party, because they have no opportunity to combine their support with that of any other candidate or party. There is no second round in an American presidential election. Simple pluralities on the first and only round determine our presidents. The American system clearly calls for a different strategy.

The History of Democratic Presidential Primaries (and Caucuses)

The 1912 presidential election produced an astounding result. Not only did the Republicans lose the White House for the first time in twenty years, to Woodrow Wilson, but their candidate, the incumbent President William Taft finished third behind his predecessor Theodore Roosevelt, who had bolted the party and attempted to return to the White House as the Progressive Party candidate. For the first time since the party's arrival on the national scene in 1856, the Republican candidate had failed to finish in the top two. And the surprises went even a little deeper. In fourth place, there was Socialist Eugene Debs with 6% of the vote, making this the first race with four presidential candidates with over 5%. The Prohibitionist Party candidate also got better than 1%, as the Prohibitionists generally did in those days, making it the first race with five candidates with at least one percentage point of the vote. It seemed that the Democrat/Republican duopoly that had dominated American politics for the past half century might be giving way to a new formation at the top.

Obviously this did not happen. By 1916 Roosevelt returned to the Republican fold, the Republican candidate finished second again, and no one but a Democrat or a Republican has cracked the top two since. Never again has a fourth place finisher matched Debs's success, nor has there been another election with five candidates finishing with better than 1%. And yet there was a development in the 1912 race that would lead to a profound change in the way that America chose its presidents, although its full impact would not be realized for another sixty years. Before bolting to form the Progressive Party, Roosevelt challenged Taft in a series of Republican Party presidential primaries, the first time these elections would play a significant role in the nominating process.

For the first few U.S. presidential elections, during the so-called "Era of Good Feelings," presidential candidates were simply chosen in congressional caucuses. In 1831 the Anti-Masonic Party became the first to hold a convention, a device previously utilized in nominating local candidates, to choose a presidential nominee. The two "major" parties of the day quickly followed suit and the next year, incumbent Andrew Jackson became the first president so nominated when the Democratic Party convention chose him to run for a second term. Nominating conventions have remained with us ever since.

Primary elections are often recalled as a legacy of the Progressive movement that advocated them – along with other reforms such as initiative, referendum and recall elections and the direct election of U.S. Senators – in order to wrest power from both political machines and capitalist interests like the railroads. But while there is substantial truth to this generalization – particularly insofar as bringing them into the presidential nominating process goes, the fact is that primaries date back at least as far as 1842 when the Democratic Party of Crawford County, Pennsylvania utilized this procedure.[12]

By 1888 the use of the primary was sufficiently widespread for the British statesman James Bryce to tell his countrymen that Americans had adopted "the novel and drastic method of turning what had been a (private) party meeting into a (public) election (by polling) at which the citizens should be entitled to vote (a) for the selection of party candidates, (b) for the selection of delegates to a party Convention, (c) for the members of the local party Committee. All this has now been done in practically every State, though with an endless variety of details in the provisions of the various State laws. ... This legal recognition of Party as a public political institution, this application of statutory regulation to what had theretofore been purely voluntary and extra-legal associations of citizens, strikes Europeans as a surprising new departure in politics. American reformers, however, had been so long accustomed to regard their parties as great political forces, national institutions which for good or for ill ruled the course of politics, that ... Nothing weaker than the arm of the law seemed to them

History of Democratic Presidential Primaries

capable of democratizing that nominating machinery which had been worked by a selfish oligarchy."[13]

The use of this uniquely American institution in the presidential nominating process was still a few years in the future, however. Florida Democrats held the first primary for selecting presidential nominating convention delegates in 1904, but those delegates were not pledged to a specific candidate. The first primary to actually pit presidential candidates against each other occurred in Ohio in 1908, when Secretary of War and President-to-be William Taft won his home state over its Governor, Joseph Foraker. Three further primary contests were held between committed delegate slates, with Taft winning one and favorite sons the other two. Wisconsin also held a Democratic primary, won by eventual third-time nominee William Jennings Bryan, who had himself been promoting the primary idea for some time.

The method of choosing delegates to national conventions was generally a matter left up to the various state parties and eventually, in some cases, state law. In 1912, 13 state Republican parties opted for primaries. Roosevelt's nine wins included Taft's home state of Ohio. The president won but two and left-wing Senator Robert La Follette won two, including his home state of Wisconsin, as he had four years earlier. Roosevelt gained a 271-71 delegate advantage over Taft in the primary states, with La Follette at 41, but these delegates did not constitute the majority at the convention and Taft pulled all the levers of power available to him to secure the nomination.

On the Democratic side, the 1912 nomination fight is primarily remembered for the 46 ballots it took New Jersey Governor Woodrow Wilson to prevail over U.S. House Speaker Champ Clark of Missouri – who led for the first 30 ballots. The two had each won several head-to-head primary match-ups leading up to the convention, but primaries were not then decisive in the Democrats' process either. In his first State of the Union address, Wilson embraced "the prompt enactment of legislation which will provide for primary elections throughout the country at which the voters of the several parties may choose their nominees for the Presidency without the intervention of nominating conventions." Conventions, he suggested might be limited to "the purpose of declaring and accepting the verdict of the primaries and formulating the platforms of the parties." That would not come to pass, but in 1916 both the Democrats and Republicans did choose a majority of their delegates via primary.[14]

But the 1916 primaries produced little of interest, as the Democrats backed their incumbent and the reunited Republicans didn't produce compelling candidates. So the shift to primaries proved less popular, and more expensive, than envisioned. Some felt that these intraparty contests contributed to debilitating factionalism. The number of primaries was cut back in subsequent elections and they would not again determine a majority of convention delegates until 1972.

These early "major party" primary races were not a focal point for the American left which still mainly looked to the third party route – Debs as well as Farmer-Labor candidate Parley Christensen in 1920, then the 1924 Robert La Follette candidacy run under the rubric of a new Progressive Party, organizationally unconnected to Roosevelt's organization. But in 1928, the third party option virtually disappeared, as the Socialists failed to bounce back from their endorsement of La Follette's campaign. With Debs and La Follette dead, the party turned to Presbyterian clergyman Norman Thomas for the first of his six presidential runs. Not only did the party's presidential vote drop under 1% for the first time in its history, but the overall "non-major" party vote sank to 1.08%, its lowest level since 1872. And this year proved more the rule than an aberration: Since then, only four third party presidential candidates of the left have exceeded 1% of the vote – Thomas in 1932, William Lemke in 1936 (and, as we have see, even calling him a candidate of the left is controversial), Henry Wallace in 1948 and Ralph Nader, whose 2.7% in 2000 stands as the largest left wing third party vote since La Follette.

Nor were the left's independent political efforts immediately replaced by developments inside the big two parties. No politician espousing views similar to La Follette's would ever again enjoy similar standing in the Republican Party. While the Democrats held interesting primary contests, no reliably identifiable candidate of the left participated in either the 1928 or 1932 races. But the increase in primary voter participation was substantial – 1.3 million participated in the 1928 Democratic Party

History of Democratic Presidential Primaries

presidential primaries; by 1932 the number was 3 million. And a reasonable argument can be made that 1932 was the year the center of gravity of the American left, as broadly defined throughout this book, shifted into the Democratic party. This argument is a retroactive one, however, in the sense that the presidential candidate Franklin Roosevelt who won the majority of the year's 16 Democratic primaries was quite different than the President Franklin Roosevelt of historical memory. The 1932 FDR was anything but a caution-be-damned, government-must-seize-the-day sort of candidate. Rather than the New Deal programs, the defense of which would later become a rallying point for the left, that year's party platform actually called for reduced government spending.

The Democrats' long-standing requirement that a nominee secure a two-thirds delegate majority (generally understood to give southern Democrats veto power) meant that Roosevelt won the 1932 nomination only after four ballots – and agreeing to put the segregationist Speaker of the House John Garner of Texas on the ticket. In 1936 Roosevelt's allies changed the nomination rule to a simple majority and it has remained so ever since. By this point the programs collectively known as the New Deal had emerged. Roosevelt facing only a minor intraparty challenge from his right and none at all from his left, was renominated by acclamation. The real action was on the Republican side where long-term Idaho Senator William Borah attempted to revitalize the party's progressive/liberal wing. Borah had refused to support President Herbert Hoover's reelection in 1932 and enjoyed the support of Wisconsin Senator Robert La Follette, Jr., who had succeeded his late father. Borah won the most primaries, but that counted for little as the party establishment handily nominated its choice, Kansas Governor Alf Landon. That would be the last substantial insurgency from that quarter in the Republican Party.

1940 saw Roosevelt get most of the votes in that year's 13 Democratic primaries, although not actually appearing to be a candidate. With an unparalleled two terms to develop control

The Primary Route

Henry Wallace (on right) with FDR and Harry Truman, the man who replaced him on the 1944 ticket.

over the party apparatus, his people easily managed to see to it that he was drafted to run for an unprecedented third term at the national convention. Roosevelt's 1944 renomination in the midst of the Second World War was pretty much the same story – minus the drama.   1948 was another matter entirely. Vice President Garner, who had declined to go along with Roosevelt's third term, had been replaced on the 1940 ticket by Secretary of Agriculture Henry Wallace who, although a Republican until 1936, was considered to represent the left reach of the administration.   In 1944, a group of conservative party leaders, particularly motivated by their justified fear that Roosevelt would not live through his fourth term, told the president they wanted Wallace off the ticket. Negotiations with a seemingly uncharacteristically diffident FDR produced the choice of Missouri Senator Harry Truman to replace him. Wallace would not stand down, however, and took the fight to the convention where he actually led on the first vice-presidential ballot, but Truman won on the second.

So after Roosevelt's death eighty-two days into his fourth

term, it was Truman, not Wallace, who was running for renomination and reelection in 1948. Opposition to Truman within the Democratic Party was substantial – on both the left and the right, with the hardest-core opposition on both sides opting to leave the party. Wallace, who had been reappointed to Roosevelt's Cabinet as Secretary of Commerce and served for a time in that capacity under Truman, ran as the candidate of the Progressive Party, the third unrelated campaign to use that name in the twentieth century, while segregationist South Carolina Senator Strom Thurmond ran as a "Dixiecrat," making Truman's ultimate win over New York Governor Tom Dewey all the more remarkable.

Estes Kefauver – First Democratic Presidential Primary Insurgent

While Truman's upset reelection victory no doubt muted recriminations on the electoral front, the left faced the far harsher charge that it was Communist-dominated and, therefore, an agent of the Soviet Union. Certainly the tendency to split from the Democratic Party was greatly muted on the left in 1952. The Progressive Party did field another presidential candidate, Vincent Hallinan, but his vote was a small percentage of Wallace's. There was, however, a serious challenge from within the party, in the person of Tennessee Senator Estes Kefauver, whose 1951 Senate hearings on organized crime had arguably made him the nation's first political television star. In his book, *The Fifties,* David Halberstam wrote that "Estes Kefauver came off as a sort of Southern Jimmy Stewart, the lone citizen-politician who gets tired of the abuse of government and goes off on his own to do something about it."[15] Arguably also the first modern shake-every-hand-out-there presidential candidate, Kefauver entered the New Hampshire primary and beat Harry Truman. And there was no mistaking the voters' intent, since state law had recently changed and primary voters now cast ballots for the actual presidential candidates, rather than their proxies.

Estes Kefauver, first modern presidential campaigner.

Following this defeat, Truman announced that he was not a candidate for reelection. He would later maintain that he had already decided against seeking a second full term, but in any case the fact was that a sitting president eligible for reelection had withdrawn following a setback in the New Hampshire primary, just as Lyndon Johnson would do 16 years later. Kefauver went on to clean up in that year's primaries, winning 12 of 15 and drawing 65% of the overall vote against a field of comers that included various favorite sons and, briefly, the incumbent president. As a result, when the Democrats arrived for their Chicago nominating convention, Kefauver led the pack. But he had not secured the nomination. Only 39% of the convention delegates had been chosen in the primaries and Kefauver had but 28% of the delegates on the first ballot at what would prove to be the last major party nominating convention requiring multiple ballots to pick a

History of Democratic Presidential Primaries

presidential nominee. Republican President-to-be Dwight Eisenhower had also recently become a second-ballot nominee at the Republican convention. Kefauver actually upped his total a bit on the second round but as he said, "The boys in the smoke-filled rooms have never taken very well to me." Much less remembered today than Illinois Governor Adlai Stevenson, the man whom party regulars would draft and put over the top on the third ballot, Kefauver might not exactly fit the profile of a left candidate, but would likely have been the more popular choice among readers of this book.

While 1952 did demonstrate that even sweeping the primaries would not necessarily make you the nominee, it did also show that the primaries could make you a contender, or wreck your candidacy. So in 1956 the Democratic primaries were contested as never before. Kefauver won New Hampshire again and another couple of early primaries. But Stevenson was also running again and this time he wasn't waiting to be drafted. The two would hold the first televised presidential debate and Stevenson ultimately overtook Kefauver in overall primary vote, although not in number of primaries won, with his big victory in California, which caused Kefauver to withdraw from campaigning before the convention.[16] The 1956 nomination was for all intents and purposes won in the primaries, even though only 38% of the delegates were chosen there.

Although considered a frontrunner for 1960, Kefauver took himself out of consideration in 1959. But the man he beat for the 1956 vice presidential nomination was back for the 1960 run, when roughly the same proportion of the delegates would be chosen via primary. Kennedy took 10 out of 15 of them on his way to winning the nomination, but it was those where he defeated Hubert Humphrey head-on – Wisconsin and West Virginia – that were considered decisive.

By 1964, primaries chose 46% of the Democratic delegates. There was, however, an incumbent Democratic President, Lyndon Johnson, whose only primary challenge came from the right, in the person of Alabama Governor George Wallace. Wallace ran better than expected against three separate Johnson surrogate candidates outside of the deep south, but the nomination was a foregone conclusion and LBJ was nominated by acclamation, as FDR had

The Primary Route

been in 1936.

Even though the percentage of Democratic primary delegates actually declined a bit in 1968, this was the campaign that would transform the primaries into the central events in the nominating process that they are today. Since Johnson had served less than half of John Kennedy's term after his assassination, he was eligible for a second full term. And again being an incumbent, he remained the natural favorite. But he had expanded the Vietnam War beyond a breaking point. From the 16,000 troops deployed there in 1963, the number of American military personnel sent to Vietnam swelled to over 536,000 in 1968, while the annual American death count grew from 118 to 16,592 over those years. And in early 1968 the Vietnamese Tet offensive had put the lie to American commanding officer General William Westmoreland's claim, made only ten weeks earlier, that there was "light at the end of the tunnel."

The antiwar challenge was taken up by Minnesota Senator Eugene McCarthy who, while personally not at all the sort of campaigner that Estes Kefauver had been, brought something to the race that Kefauver had not – a burgeoning base of young antiwar activists and prominent antiwar entertainers like movie star Paul Newman who were surfacing in numbers not seen since before the McCarthy-era Hollywood Red Scare. McCarthy took 42% of the New Hampshire primary vote. He did not win – the president got 49% – but it was just as good: he did actually take 20 of the state's 24 delegates because his backers ran a unified slate rather than running against each other, as Johnson supporters had. Four days later, New York Senator Robert Kennedy, who had previously declined "Dump Johnson" movement organizer Allard Lowenstein's entreaties to run before the movement turned to McCarthy, now entered the race. Two weeks after that, Johnson bowed out. A month later, Vice President Hubert Humphrey was in.   On June 4, the night that Kennedy was assassinated, he had just beaten McCarthy 46% to 42% in the California primary, won South Dakota and lost New Jersey. McCarthy had tallied more overall primary votes but, as had been the case for every convention except 1916, most delegates were not chosen in primaries and Kennedy led McCarthy by 393 to 258 in the head

Gene McCarthy's 1968 antiwar "children's crusade" enjoyed an unprecedented level of youth participation.

count. But it was Humphrey, who had not, and would not, run in any primaries, who held the lead at 561 delegates, gained by working the party regulars and machines. South Dakota Senator George McGovern, who actually had the best antiwar record of all of the Democrats mentioned here, but faced a difficult reelection campaign that year and had therefore also previously declined Allard Lowenstein's request to run, now joined the fray shortly

The Primary Route

before the party's Chicago nominating convention. Many of Kennedy's supporters had developed an antipathy for McCarthy in the heat of the race and McGovern attempted to offer them another antiwar option. Some people even printed up "George McGovern is the real Gene McCarthy" buttons, alluding to McGovern's superior antiwar record. There was even a move to nominate Massachusetts Senator Edward Kennedy, to which McCarthy acceded, but it came to nought. Although antiwar candidates had taken nearly 70% of the primary vote, the pro-war Humphrey had over two-thirds of the delegates on the first ballot.

The antiwar frustration was ferocious, both outside the convention, where Chicago police beat demonstrators in full view of the nation's television watchers, and inside, where McCarthy and Kennedy backers attempted to amend the party's election platform with an antiwar plank calling for an immediate end to the bombing of North Vietnam. Not surprisingly, they failed, drawing the support of only 40% of the delegates and ensuring that the vast and growing antiwar sector of the population felt they had no place to turn in November.

The generally unsuccessful insurgents did enjoy one convention success, however. The one minority report that carried the day called for a study of revamping the party's delegate selection rules, a study that resulted in the number of delegates chosen in primaries shooting up to 65% in 1972, then to 72% by 1980. The number subsequently declined but then reached a new high of 77% in 1992. It has since never dropped below 60%, a level never reached before 1972. And although its rules have differed, the Republican Party has largely been caught up in the push for greater use of primaries as well. Perhaps the clearest measure of their importance in the recent era is the fact that since 1972 only once has a major party convention, the Republicans in 1976, convened without the identity of the nominee already being clear.

George McGovern – the Insurgent Wins

George McGovern was chosen as the compromise candidate to run the commission created by the 1968 convention resolution on reforming the delegate selection process, which

History of Democratic Presidential Primaries

would come to be known as the McGovern-Fraser Commission. The commission's report, *Mandate for Reform,* proposed rules for the democratic selection of delegates; greater representation of minorities, women and youth; and a reduction in the influence of party bosses. The implementation of the changes would eventually mean that while the political deck obviously remained stacked against the "little people" – those without significant wealth or power – it might at least be no more so within the Democratic Party than within the electoral process as a whole.

McGovern would utilize the new rules to great effect after resigning from the commission and announcing his candidacy for president. 1968 vice presidential nominee Edmund Muskie was the early favorite of the party establishment, but his candidacy quickly unraveled and the insider baton again passed to 1968 presidential nominee Humphrey. Although Humphrey would ultimately win a slightly higher number of overall primary votes, McGovern beat him eleven states to four. Neither of them were that far ahead of Alabama Governor George Wallace in total votes.

McGovern was a serious antiwar candidate. During a 1970 Senate debate, he had declared that "Every senator in this chamber is partly responsible for sending 50,000 young Americans to an early grave. This chamber reeks of blood."[17] In his nomination acceptance speech McGovern pledged to have every American soldier and POW back home within ninety days of taking office. He had elsewhere declared that, "It is the establishment center that has led us into the stupidest and cruelest war in all history."[18] This was not the liberal wing of the "establishment center" that had won the nomination and the establishment center knew this, and didn't like it one bit. As McGovern saw it twenty years later, "The 1972 campaign wasn't simply against our Vietnam policy, but a fundamental challenge to the Cold War and the whole apparatus that supported it, including excessive military spending and the militarization of our economy and society. We haven't had that kind of challenge since."[19]

McGovern proposed a Fiscal Year 1975 military budget of $54.8 billion – $32 billion lower than Nixon administration projections. But the differences went far beyond those numbers. As the candidate saw it, "This election ... is a fundamental struggle

105

The Primary Route

between the little people of America and the big rich of America, between the average working man or woman and the powerful elite."[20] At the same time, it is true that for the candidate, as well as for the core of his campaign, the Vietnam War was *the* issue. But while Vietnamese continued to suffer under increased American bombardment (as did Cambodians and Laotians bombed in our "secret" wars), domestically, Nixon's "Vietnamization" of the war had succeeded in making it not nearly the issue that it had been in 1968. Although American soldiers suffered their second highest casualty total of the war years during Nixon's first year in office, 11,780, and more than a third of all American Vietnam War deaths would occur during his first term, by 1972, the number of American casualties was at its lowest level – 759 – since 1964, as was the overall troop deployment of 24,200.

Nixon, of course, would turn out to be the only president ever to resign, after his campaign's break-in at the Democratic Party headquarters in the Watergate complex in Washington, DC was exposed and the president turned out to indeed be the "crook" he had denied being. The shift in public attitudes that followed the Watergate Hearings was so drastic that in August, 1973 NBC pollsters found a majority of voters saying they would elect McGovern if the vote were held today.[21] There the moment seemed to hold great "I told you so" political turnaround potential – but it did not materialize.

The reasons for McGovern's loss – by a 61-38% margin, almost identical to that of Arizona Senator Barry Goldwater's loss to Lyndon Johnson in 1964 – have been discussed and debated ever since. Certainly the choice and subsequent withdrawal of vice presidential nominee Missouri Senator Thomas Eagleton figured large, as did the refusal to support McGovern by mainline party figures who found their influence diminished by the delegate-selection rules changes. The most significant organizational abstention came from the AFL-CIO. The labor federation's failure to endorse McGovern was one of only two instances since Woodrow Wilson's first campaign that the labor federation declined to support the Democratic nominee, the other being the organization's endorsement of La Follette when he ran to the left of the Democrats in 1924.

History of Democratic Presidential Primaries

Unlike the situation of the Republican right which dug in and redoubled its efforts after Goldwater's loss, the McGovern defeat clearly demoralized the Democratic electoral left. To be sure, the Democratic left never enjoyed the kind of financial support that saw the Republican right through its dark years. And yet it's hard to avoid concluding that a substantial number of McGovern backers decided not just that mistakes were made, but that the whole thing had been a mistake: a candidate that good on the issues simply couldn't be elected president and therefore they had been wrong to try. This failure of will may stand as the greatest single shortcoming in the all-too-modest history of the American electoral left.

Shirley Chisholm

It's a mark of how tumultuous the period was that Shirley Chisholm's 1972 presidential campaign has largely been lost in the historical glare. But it was the rare year that had some people on the left arguing not over which candidate was "the lesser of two evils," but which was the greater of two goods. When Chisholm announced for president in January of that year, calling for a "bloodless revolution" at the nominating convention, the Brooklyn Congresswoman became the first black woman to run for president and the first woman of any race to seek the Democratic nomination. Opposing the Vietnam War, she supported a minimum family income, championed the Equal Rights Amendment and civil rights legislation, and opposed wiretapping and domestic spying.

She faced continual questioning about the "meaning" or "purpose" of her candidacy and coming from as far from the mainstream of standard campaign operations as it did, her campaign was poorly funded and organized. Chisholm later said she'd do it quite differently if she had it to do all over again. Of course the same could be said of many of the campaigns of the left that we'll run across. Chisholm's best showing came in North Carolina – 7.5% and third place. She also finished fourth in California at 4.4%. She won a total of 20 delegates, but after it became clear that he could not stop McGovern's candidacy, Hubert Humphrey gave his blessing, enabling his delegates to cast their ballots for her and she actually received 152 votes at the

BRING U.S. TOGETHER

VOTE CHISHOLM 1972

UNBOUGHT AND UNBOSSED

Shirley Chisholm, the first woman to seek the Democratic nomination.

convention. There've been many other years when a campaign that the candidate described as running "in spite of hopeless odds ... to demonstrate the sheer will and refusal to accept the status quo" might have qualified as the left's beacon of hope. But coming when it did, to the extent that people discuss her campaign at all, it is primarily as a precursor, first to the Jackson campaign and then to the Clinton-Obama race.

History of Democratic Presidential Primaries

Back to Normal

At first it did seem like things might continue on from the McGovern campaign (and the Chisholm campaign) when former Oklahoma Senator Fred Harris picked up the torch in 1976. Harris, a 1968 Humphrey supporter who as chairman of the Democratic National Committee had nominated all of the members of the McGovern-Fraser Commission, had actually declared his candidacy for the 1972 nomination. His effort lasted a mere seven weeks, however, before he ran out of money, raising the question at the time of whether a poor person really could run for president. He did promote a platform amendment to strip deductions and exemptions from the federal tax code which actually appeared to carry the day at that year's national convention – the Wallace delegates liked it – but was gavelled to defeat by the McGovern forces who did not want their candidate to have run on a platform advocating the elimination of the home mortgage deduction.

As a result of the 1971 adoption of the Twenty-sixth Amendment to the United States Constitution, 18-20 year-old voters had joined the presidential electorate for the first time in 1972. And on top of that, the 1976 election would be the first one conducted under new federal campaign finance legislation that many hoped would weaken big money's grip on the government. So for some, anti-establishment hopes actually burned even brighter, despite the overwhelming 1972 defeat. Harris himself considered the new campaign funding law "the most massive change in politics in my lifetime." A legitimately anti-establishment-oriented politician who called his ideas the "New Populism," Harris wished to break up monopolies and replace the current system of "graduated loopholes" with a true graduated income tax. He seemed to be a quite reasonable successor to McGovern, the man so many now apparently wished they had voted for.

On top of that, Harris actually appeared to have a real campaign plan with a thought-through caucus/primary scenario. In 1975, he campaigned through 13 states traveling in a camper with his wife and daughter. His backers included Service Employees International Union president George Hardy, who had led the pro-McGovern union effort when the AFL-CIO declined to do it in 1972, and Norman Lear, producer of *All In the Family*,

109

which had given the world Archie Bunker, the nation's most famous working class television character since *The Honeymooners'* Ralph Cramden. Harris maintained that "the widespread diffusion of economic and political power ought to be the express goal—the stated goal—of government." He advocated serious cuts in military spending, the creation of two million new local government jobs to employ the unemployed, price controls on non-competitive industries, a public corporation to develop America's energy resources and nationalization of the railways.

But long shot upstart that he was, Harris was upstaged by an another, arguably even longer shot upstart when he finished behind Georgia Governor Jimmy Carter and Indiana Senator Birch Bayh, in the Iowa Caucuses – as well as "Uncommitted" which led all choices. Harris then lost further ground when he finished behind not only those two in the New Hampshire primary, but behind Arizona Congressman Morris Udall, as well. That was pretty much it for his campaign. And with him went all talk about big changes in the direction of government that year, as Democratic voters opted for Carter, who in 1972 had given the principal nominating convention speech for Washington Senator Henry Jackson, the most right wing of the Democratic Party candidates in the field.

Carter's centrist approach was not universally well received within his own party, though, and in 1980 he found his renomination challenged by Edward Kennedy. California Governor Jerry Brown also entered the race, as he had in 1976. Brown's stance was often perceived as "radical," but Kennedy was actually probably the more liberal of the two in terms of specific issues. Neither had a lot to say about foreign policy and no candidate of Harris's stripe emerged, perhaps because the presence of these two big-name candidates to Carter's left seemed to leave little room for such a candidacy.

The most lasting effect of Kennedy's run, however, followed as it was by Carter's loss to Ronald Reagan in November, repeating the Republican experience of 1976 when Reagan challenged sitting President Gerald Ford who then lost to Carter, may have been to render challenges to sitting Democratic presidents *verboten.* A left wing commentator would later write

History of Democratic Presidential Primaries

that Kennedy "weakened Carter badly and helped paved [sic] the way for the landslide election of Ronald Reagan, by far a greater threat to Kennedy's liberal values than Carter."[22] After Carter's renomination, Kennedy even declined to make the traditional gesture of joining and raising hands together on the convention stage.

In 1984, George McGovern made a now largely forgotten reentry into the presidential field, running on a platform of major military spending cuts, immediate military withdrawal from Lebanon and Central America, and a significant public works program. His announcement speech declared that, "It is no longer possible at acceptable cost for either Washington or Moscow to impose its will against the revolutionary currents of Central America, Afghanistan, Southeast Asia, Poland, Africa and the Middle East." McGovern, who had lost his Senate seat in the Reagan election in 1980, pulled off a surprise third-place finish in the Iowa caucuses, ahead of California Senator Alan Cranston, previously considered the "peace candidate." Coming from an agribusiness state, Cranston had failed to appreciate the continuing relevance of farm parity as an issue in the mid-west, something with which the South Dakotan McGovern was quite familiar. He dropped from the race, however, when he could do no better than third in the primary in Massachusetts, the only state he had carried against Nixon twelve years earlier.

Jesse Jackson – There Is a Left!

Civil rights leader Jesse Jackson also entered the 1984 race. Although by the time McGovern withdrew Jackson had yet to match McGovern's 21% in Massachusetts, a subsequent 26% third-place finish in New York established the seriousness of Jackson's base – African-American and left wing voters who were undaunted by the fact that he had no realistic prospect of ultimately winning the nomination. He later won the Louisiana and District of Columbia primaries with a program advocating a broad shift from foreign military spending toward domestic social needs. Jackson supported major military spending cuts, a revived Works Progress Administration-style infrastructure project, a single-payer health care system and reparations to the descendants of slaves. Although he did serious damage to his candidacy with an

The Primary Route

anti-Jewish slur during the New York campaign, he took 21% of the overall national primary vote. He got 465 votes at the convention, a much smaller percentage than his share of the vote, but a surprise to the mainstream, nonetheless.

In 1988, he came back bigger and better. The campaign was smoother, the gaffes fewer – although his previous New York primary remarks had marked him for permanent opposition by some – and Jackson took 29% of the overall primary vote and about that percentage of convention delegates, in contrast to 1984 when he won but 8% of them.

But then what? In two runs, Jackson had established that a candidate with an African-American base running on a platform of the left might find a significant core of support. At the end of his first campaign, he had even established an ongoing organization, the Rainbow Coalition, that was designed to continue work on the campaign's issues outside of the campaign structure and schedule. At the same time, few thought that his campaigns could ultimately result in victory, for him or anyone bearing the organization's standard. So in 1992, when he opted against a third run, no one filled the void.

There was the question of who had standing to run for president. Since 1932, with one exception, Presidents-elect have previously held the office of vice-president, U.S. Senator, or governor, the exception being Dwight Eisenhower, formerly Supreme Commander of Allied Forces in World War II. Those who tried and fell short, but were considered serious contenders in the process, had also largely come from similar electoral backgrounds. Jackson, however, had never held political office. Yet his unique standing in the black community allowed him to run ahead of candidates who did have the normally requisite offices in their past.

Chances are that you have never heard of Larry Agran – and therein lies the short story of the left in the 1992 presidential campaign. Agran was actually the most prominent candidate of the left to attempt to carry the torch that year, running on a platform that called for withdrawing permanent U.S. troops from Europe and Japan, cutting the defense budget by half and redirecting the savings to local revenue sharing, additional funding for public

History of Democratic Presidential Primaries

education, a national health-care program and environmental projects. Unlike Jackson, Agran had actually held office, but nothing higher than mayor of Irvine, California, the largest planned city in the country – an affluent, mostly Republican, University of California-campus city with a population under 150,000.

Agran's highpoint in the entire race was arguably a January 22, 1992 poll that put his support at 8%, in a three-way tie for third place. But unlike the other two candidates with whom he was tied, former California Governor Jerry Brown and Iowa Senator Tom Harkin, the modest nature of his electoral resume allowed him to be dismissed as a less-than-serious candidate by the media. Barred from presidential debates, he was even once arrested for trying to enter the location where one of the debates was being held. His best primary showing was only 1.6% in Idaho; he received three votes at the convention.

For the left, what the race firmly established was that there was a "notoriety floor" for presidential campaigns – a required level of prior recognition that was necessary to prevent one's campaign from being entirely submerged by a hostile political establishment and a skeptical-to-querulous journalistic establishment. The 1995 documentary film, *Spin,* covers the story of the media's refusal to cover Agran. Where the chants of "Run, Jesse, Run" had overridden the continual questioning of "What does Jesse want?" nothing kept Agran from being totally ignored in the campaign's news coverage. Harkin was the most liberal of the candidates to draw any serious attention, but he withdrew before the Super Tuesday primaries, leaving the field to eventual winner Bill Clinton, the business-oriented former Massachusetts Senator Paul Tsongas, and Brown who, one conservative commentator noted, simultaneously "seemed to be the most left-wing and right-wing man in the field."[23]

No candidate of the left appeared to challenge incumbent Bill Clinton in the 1996 Democratic primaries, perhaps not surprising, given the general perception that Kennedy's challenge had played a role in Ronald Reagan's unseating Jimmy Carter. The failure of one to appear in 2000, however, was another matter. Not even a Larry Agran entered the field – the only serious challenge to eventual nominee Vice President Al Gore came from the equally mainstream New Jersey Senator Bill Bradley. Never before had

113

The Primary Route

the Democratic Party fielded such a narrow range of options in a year without a Democratic incumbent. The two would combine for 96% of the primary vote, with about half of the rest going to lunatic fringe candidate Lyndon LaRouche, who actually took 22% in Arkansas as the only alternative to Gore.[24]

It might be a stretch to assert that there has been any real "tradition" of Democratic primary candidates of the left, but from 1968-1988, Gene McCarthy, Robert Kennedy, George McGovern, Fred Harris, Ted Kennedy and Jesse Jackson had certainly made some widely audible noise. But with that stretch now a dozen years in the past, in 2000 the focal point for electorally-oriented activists shifted back to the third party option for the first time since the 1948 Henry Wallace campaign. Ralph Nader had made a couple of desultory Democratic primary efforts in 1988 and 1992 and a somewhat more serious third party effort that finished fourth with 0.7% in 1996. While he had never held political office, his career as a consumer activist with a long string of demonstrable accomplishments had made him a household name, comparable in magnitude to Jesse Jackson. His candidacy, centered on an emerging Green Party, was clearly his most organized effort yet and offered the only visible-above-the-horizon challenge to the national status quo to come from the left since Jackson in 1988.

Debate on the impact of the Nader campaign continues to this day. Al Gore clearly won the popular nationwide vote and reasonable evidence suggests that he would have won it in Florida – and with it the Electoral College – had his campaign successfully pursued a recount statewide instead of just in four counties.[25] But one poll suggested that the absence of Nader on the ballot would have given Gore the win in Florida, even with this unfortunate recount decision. What was clear, however, was that it would be extremely difficult for any third party presidential challenger to mount a serious effort in 2004, in the face of the widespread perception/accusation that Nader had been the "spoiler" who turned the White House over to George W. Bush.

The electorally-inclined left then, not surprisingly returned to the Democratic Party race in 2004. With Massachusetts Senator John Kerry, the eventual presidential nominee, and North Carolina Senator John Edwards, who became the vice presidential nominee

History of Democratic Presidential Primaries

after first contending for the top spot himself, having both voted for the Bush Administration's post-9/11 wars in Afghanistan and, more controversially, in Iraq, former Vermont Governor Howard Dean became an early anti-Iraq-War front runner. While generally a bit to the left of the men who would be nominated – he supported creating a government-subsidized health insurance program along the lines of the later, so-called "Obamacare," as well as undoing the Bush tax cuts for the top brackets – he was no radical. His campaign faltered early and he was not prepared to run a wire-to-wire race. That role fell to Cleveland, Ohio's past mayor and then current Congressman Dennis Kucinich, who supporters asserted *"is* the candidate people *think* Howard Dean is."

Kucinich ran on a platform similar to that of Nader and Jackson before him: a Canadian-style "single payer" health care system, major military budget cuts, and fervent opposition to the Iraq War. And he was prepared to – and did – go all the way to the convention, but he never really passed the media's laugh test. Was it presumptuous for a rank-and-file, non-leadership House member to run for the White House? Kucinich ran in 49 states plus the District of Columbia and made some decent showings in caucus states, but he did not record a double digit primary vote total until two late ones when Kerry had the nomination locked up. Kucinich won 64 delegates, most of whom went with it to the end and actually cast their ballots for him at the convention, the only delegates to vote for someone other than nominee John Kerry. Those 37 delegates represented less than 1% of the total at the party convention.

Al Sharpton also ran the race until the end, although he only contested half of the states. Running on a platform similar to Kucinich's, he attempted to repeat the Jesse Jackson, outsider-civil-rights-leader candidacy, but was less successful than even Kucinich, winning 20 delegates who dispersed at the convention.

The Primary Route

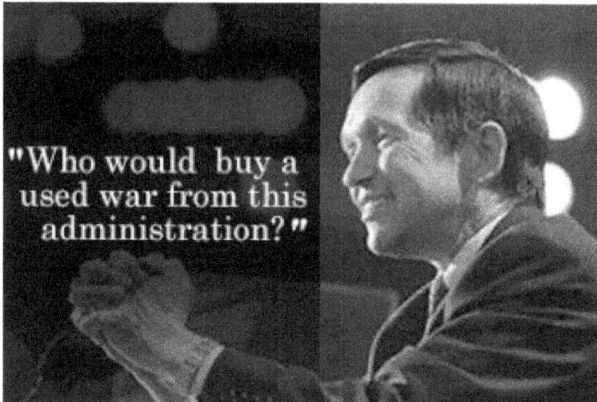

"Who would buy a used war from this administration?" *Dennis Kucinich ran two radically antiwar campaigns.*

A watershed moment for both campaigns, as well as that of former Illinois Senator Carol Moseley Braun, who withdrew early, came even before the election year started, on December 10, 2003, when the American Broadcasting Company (ABC) pulled its correspondents from coverage of all three candidates.

Kucinich tried again in 2008, but with little real 2004 success to build on, he fell to the 1992 Larry Agran plateau when he was shut out of televised debates and was out of this race by January 24. Former Alaska Senator Mike Gravel also ran on a set of issues similar to Kucinich's, to virtually no notice. And in 2012, there was no serious challenge mounted to the incumbent President Barack Obama. That no candidate of the left would decide to take this on was, by now, not at all surprising. By this time, however, it was not clear that any sense of urgency remained for running a presidential candidate of the left at all, regardless of who occupied the White House.

Dual Unionism: An Interesting Episode from Labor's Past

It would be impossible to say just how many potential activists have steered clear of electoral politics because they couldn't see their way clear to working within the Democratic Party. But it's easy enough to see why we've lost them. Not only don't most of the people in control of the Democratic Party share the point of view that motivates this book, they actively oppose it; the fact is that they are fundamentally committed to the status quo. Most of the top Democrats – candidates, office holders and funders alike – seem to have little-to-no problem with the ever-increasing dominance of big money in American society: maybe they believe in it, maybe the way American political campaigns operate leads them down that road.

And so far as our foreign policy of seemingly endless military spending and intervention goes, Barack Obama may not share the blame with George W. Bush for initiating the worst episode in recent American foreign interventions – the second Iraq War – yet in more ways than not the foreign policy continuity between the two administrations is pronounced. Obama attempted to maintain troops in Iraq past Bush's negotiated withdrawal date, extended and expanded the Afghanistan War, bombed Iraq, Libya, Pakistan, Somalia, Syria and Yemen, sent troops back to Iraq, and deployed U.S. Special Operations forces in over 125 foreign countries. And let's not forget that the prior Democratic President, Bill Clinton, bombed Bosnia, Iraq, Somalia, Sudan and Yugoslavia.

Many understandably conclude, then, that while the Democrats may have (belatedly) come around on civil rights or women's rights or gay rights, and may be marginally better than the Republicans on economic issues and maybe even on foreign policy, the fundamental problem is that the Democratic Party is

simply not *our* party but is, rather, part of the problem. Working within the Democratic Party, they argue, inevitably and fatally compromises anything we say or do. If we stick with them, we'll be singing in their band, and they'll be picking the songs. So we have no choice but to operate independently of the Democrats. And finding no place that feels like home, many simply turn their energies toward fields of activity other than electoral politics.

In his 2008 book, *Democrats: A Critical History*, third-party advocate Lance Selfa called the Democratic Party, "one of the chief pillars of the system that perpetuates exploitation and oppression" [26] and concluded that there is no substitute for *"building a political alternative to the Democrats"*[27] (italics in original). In a 2012 introduction to a new edition of the book, Selfa went on to describe various "Democratic 'betrayals'" as "the inevitable outcome of a political institution that socialists have long described as a capitalist party that only pretends to be a friend of working people."[28]

As we know, it's difficult to find political systems elsewhere in the world that are sufficiently comparable to provide us with any insight on operating within our own system. There was once, however, a debate within the American labor movement whose outlines were similar enough to the recurrent third party/Democratic Party argument that it warrants a closer look

The *Dual Unionism* Question

In the early days of labor organizing, both in this country and around the world, really – the question of unions' ultimate *purpose* was a wide open one. The central point of contention was the extent to which unions should aim to change the entire economic and political order. For the "pure and simple" unionists of the day, like Samuel Gompers, the answer was clearly that unions existed to improve the wages and working conditions of their members and should have no broader political agenda. For the socialists, a considerable force in the founding of the labor movement, it was equally obvious that unions should work for an overall transfer of power from the capitalist class to the working class. For them, the question then arose: Could the two groups, the socialists and the "pure and simples," work together in the same union? Should they?

An Interesting Episode from Labor's Past

Dual unionism is a term that has meant different things to different people at different times – some of its usages being virtually the opposite to the way it's used here – but in these pages it specifically refers to the policy of establishing alternative unions separate and distinct from the established mainstream unions. The idea was that the new unions would be more radical or militant than the already existing ones and, crucially, would be controlled by people committed to overhauling the dominant economic and political system and not to preserving it.

In the late nineteenth century, when all unions were pretty much new, it very much an open question as to just which of them would become the "established" unions. The first union that most of us encountered in our American history textbooks, the Knights of Labor, was founded in 1869 and peaked in 1886, with perhaps 700,000 members. By 1890, when its membership had already dropped below 100,000, the organization was eclipsed by the American Federation of Labor (AFL), which, unlike the Knights, was an alliance of separate unions that organized workers in particular jobs or crafts, e.g., carpenters, teamsters.

The American Railway Union (ARU), became the largest union in the country for a time in 1893-94. The ARU, headed by Eugene Debs – later to make five runs as a socialist presidential candidate – was an "industrial union." Instead of the separate railroad brotherhoods, unions that existed for the various jobs on the railroad, the ARU organized the whole industry, engineers, conductors, clerks and all, into one union. The ARU's rapid rise and fall centered on the 1894 Pullman Strike, widely referred to as the "Debs Rebellion, suppressed by the intervention of 20,000 federal troops. The AFL and the brotherhoods, most of which eventually joined the AFL, emerged as the dominant unions and *dual unionism* emerged as a recurrent issue on the left.

Samuel Gompers, the first AFL president, once addressed the question of what labor wanted: "We want more schoolhouses and less jails; more books and less arsenals; more learning and less vice; more leisure and less greed; more justice and less revenge; in fact, more of the opportunities to cultivate our better

The establishment press did not approve of the 1894 Pullman strike.

natures."[29] No one in the labor movement was likely to disagree with Gompers's prescription, but for the socialists and other militants this formulation simply didn't go far enough. As Gompers saw the divide between the socialists and the "pure and simple" unionists that he came to typify, "We recognize the poverty, we know the sweatshop, we can play on every string of the harp, and touch the tenderest chords of human sympathy; but while we recognize the evil and would apply the remedy, our Socialist friends would look forward to the promised land, and wait for 'the sweet by-and-by.' Their statements as to economic ills are right;

An Interesting Episode from Labor's Past

their conclusions and their philosophy are all askew."[30]

This sentiment was pretty much mutual, so far as the socialists and the other labor radicals went. But there was not unanimity among them on the question of what to do about the labor movement's diverging views on its fundamental purposes. Should those on the left continue to "bore from within" organizations that had leaders like Gompers who were openly hostile to their point of view? Or should they strike out on their own and create new unions more amenable to their more expansive views about the role of unions in society? Daniel DeLeon, a well-known nineteenth century socialist, stated the rationale for the latter point of view: "These pure and simple organizations are forts in the hands of the capitalist class, because these forts are held by the labor lieutenants of the capitalists."[31]

This was no idle opinion. In 1895, the Socialist Labor Party (SLP), which DeLeon headed, resolved to create a "New Trade Unionism" and established the Socialist Trade and Labor Alliance (STLA) to challenge the AFL unions. Gompers immediately denounced the organization as "dual unionism" and, as such, a betrayal of labor solidarity. Earlier in its history the AFL might, of course, have itself been accused of the same when it challenged the Knights of Labor, but since it is the AFL that has lasted all this time, it's the STLA that's generally considered the first exemplar of American *dual unionism*.

The new federation enjoyed some modest early successes, but with its growth came a desire for greater organizational independence from the SLP. The party responded by attempting to bring the STLA unions more directly under its control in 1898. Both organizations emerged from the conflict with their relevance diminished. The STLA never seriously threatened the AFL's dominance, and the SLP itself was soon eclipsed as a political force on the left by the newly created Socialist Party.

But it wasn't just Marxist theorists like DeLeon who thought that they might be better off with a new set of unions. By the turn of the century, miners in the American west, once accustomed to working under mine owners who had themselves actually been miners at one point and therefore knew something

Daniel DeLeon set up a labor federation to rival the AFL.

about mining, now found themselves dealing with free market capital that didn't know anything about mining but knew everything about profit. As Western Federation of Miners (WFM) Secretary-Treasurer "Big Bill" Haywood put it, the mine owners "did not find the gold, they did not mine the gold, they did not mill the gold, but by some weird alchemy all the gold belonged to them!"[32]

Organizing in extremely difficult circumstances in places like Cripple Creek, Colorado, where the mine owners not only

An Interesting Episode from Labor's Past

brought in strikebreakers but recruited their own private army to break the union, the WFM found itself very much in search of allies. In 1896, the WFM affiliated with the AFL. But things didn't go too well when the hard rock miners met the forces of "organized labor of the east" at the AFL convention the following year. A later history described the miners coming away "feeling that they had not been associating with union men, or with men possessing the moral or intellectual fibre ever to become good union men" and the WFM disaffiliated.[33]

Continuing to seek affiliation with a larger organization whose conclusions about what needed to be done might be more drastic than the AFL's, the miners ultimately decided to try to create one themselves. First broadening their ranks to become the Western Federation of Labor, they then went national in 1902 as the American Labor Union (ALU). Constituting itself as a direct competitor with the AFL, the new union broke with the AFL's generally non-political stance and supported the Socialist Party.

In 1905, the ALU merged with the Industrial Workers of the World (IWW). Committed to building "one big union," instead of perpetuating the AFL's divisions into the various craft unions, this "dual union" shone far brighter than the STLA ever had. IWW campaigns constituted some of the most vivid chapters in American labor history – the free speech fights in western states; the first sit-down strike in Schenectady, New York in 1906; the 1912 Lawrence, Massachusetts "Bread and Roses" textile strike; the 1913 Paterson, New Jersey silk strike; and early farm worker organizing campaigns.

The IWW and the Socialist Party drew apart into their separate spheres of activities, but both organizations argued that the worker of one country had no business fighting the worker of another country in a war that would ultimately benefit only militarists and industrialists. Both organizations attracted a great deal of attention for their opposition to U.S. entry into World War I. Not all of the attention was welcome, however, and the organizations suffered heavily for their stance, both at the hands of vigilantes and the government, most notably in the so-called Palmer Raids ordered by Woodrow Wilson's Attorney General A. Mitchell Palmer in 1919 and 1920. The wartime and postwar repression – combined with the IWW's relatively unstable

The Primary Route

organizational structure and defections to the new Communist Party – ultimately reduced the IWW to a marginal organizing role.

The next organizational foray into dual unionism came at the end of the next decade, when the Communist Party launched the Trade Union Unity League (TUUL). Previously the American Communists had taken the same "boring from within" tack as their political rivals in the Socialist Party and most of the various other unaffiliated labor militants. But in 1929 the Communist International directed the world's Communist parties to form their own unions, with programs more radical than the mainstream unions they were currently involved with.

During this period, the Communists developed their well-deserved and ultimately unshakable reputation for acting upon orders from Moscow, regardless of what actually might make sense in America. William Z. Foster, the preeminent Communist union activist of the day, summed up the Communists' sensibility in explaining that although this shift to dual unionism flew in the face of everything he considered sensible, he decided that "as a good Communist I just have to go along."[34]

Foster's initial critical instincts proved right in the long run and this entire worldwide effort was scrapped in another Moscow-directed policy shift in 1935. While all of this had the effect of irreparably damaging the Communists' credibility, it did at least allow them to participate in American labor's greatest upsurge – the building of the CIO. The Committee for Industrial Organizing actually began as a project within the AFL to organize mass production industries along industrial lines, similar to the way the ARU had organized, although with a different union in each industry. But the unions that formed the CIO very quickly developed a "You can't fire me – I quit" relationship with the AFL and by 1936 they were out on their own.

The divorce proved to be quite successful and the unleashed CIO organizing drive ushered in an era in which American unions enjoyed the greatest strength and influence they would ever know. This success, combined with the 1955 reconnection of the AFL with what was by now called the Congress of Industrial Organizations, has meant that, although there were points where AFL and CIO unions were in direct

An Interesting Episode from Labor's Past

competition, the separate CIO years are seldom recalled as being in any way connected to the dual unionism heresy of earlier decades. This may be partially due to selective organizational memory, but it is also true that, unlike previous splits, the CIO impulse to break with the AFL derived from the Federation's perceived sloth in spreading unionism, rather from any fundamental objection to the nature of that unionism.

Certainly, by the time the great industrial organizing drives of the 1930s ended, no ideological dual union impulse of any significance had survived. So when the next significant split in the labor movement occurred in 2005, with seven unions leaving the AFL-CIO to form the Change to Win Federation, the schism had everything to do with organizing philosophy and relatively little to do with social philosophy. No one in the new Federation advocated leaving the AFL-CIO on the grounds that its leaders failed to advocate a break with the current economic system.

Today's labor movement encompasses a range of opinion as broad as that of any other period in its history. On the one side, the advocates of "pure and simple" unions are still around. They don't use that term any more, of course, but the idea's still pretty much the same: A union's job is to improve wages and working conditions – no more, no less. On the rank and file level, there are any number of union members with absolutely no interest in a radical transformation of society or even in how their union thinks they should vote. Likewise on the organizational level, some unions' involvement in politics goes no further than trying to ensure recognition of its members' interests in the legislative process. At the other end of the spectrum there are still those who see the labor movement as America's best hope for major social transformations, not only on the domestic side, but even for altering our foreign policy. And just as in labor's early days, some of them are socialists, some are anarchists, and there are even some who still call themselves communists.

What is different from labor's early days, however, is that while individuals on either side of this dichotomy might well wish that the other side would go away, and might even on occasion try to help them on their way out, there's no one actually trying to organize new unions on the basis of the argument that if you want to change the world, you can't be part of a union whose leaders support the status quo. Dual unionism as an ideological stance has totally disappeared.

In its day, dual unionism was an interesting and important theory. A great deal of thought and effort went into the various dual union campaigns, and yet over time a consensus emerged that the specific conditions of American society, law, and labor relations necessitated relegating that theory to the history books. For today's trade unionists who have a broad, social change agenda, the question has long since become not *whether* they work within unions whose leadership might not share their views on issues beyond the job, but *how* they work within them.

An analogy can never prove a point, of course. So the history of dual unionism and its eventual abandonment obviously does not prove that the America left's predilection for third parties must also be left behind. But it is a clear example of a case when a position that once seemed entirely logical – and certainly the most "radical" – had to be abandoned because it was not what the actually existing structure of American society called for.

The Democratic Presidential Nominating Convention

The presidential candidates of the modern era are expected to bear a certain entrepreneurial bent. Potential nominees *want* the job. So much so, that the intensity of their drive to secure the nomination is now widely viewed as a reasonable predictor or measure of candidates' ability – and not just their ability to win the actual election if nominated, but as evidence of their ability to govern the nation if elected.

Today, no nominee will be surprised to be nominated. There hasn't been one who didn't arrive at a convention "hell bent on election" since the Democrats nominated Adlai Stevenson for the first time in 1952. Stevenson's more-or-less draft was also the last nomination that required more than a single ballot.

Not only are there no longer any surprise nominees, but no one who fails to get the nomination is the slightest bit surprised any more, either. There hasn't been a presidential nominating convention whose outcome was still in doubt by the time it convened since incumbent Gerald Ford held off future president Ronald Reagan by a 1,187 – 1,070 margin in 1976. In fact, nowadays, if a party were to open its convention without the nominee-to-be's delegate ducks already being lined up, any number of spin doctors would no doubt brand it as a party in disarray. At the least, any such unpredictable convention would represent a serious disruption in the now decades-long trend of one convention becoming more of a political rally/infomercial than the last.

Conventions were a very different sort of event early in the twentieth century, however. When presidential primaries had their first serious impact in 1912, their presence still wasn't defining. Regardless of how a candidate might fare in the primaries of the early part of the twentieth century, there generally weren't enough delegates at stake in them to make or break a candidacy. In 1912,

The Primary Route

Speaker of the House Champ Clark of Missouri entered and won a few primaries as did New Jersey Governor Woodrow Wilson, but neither acquired anywhere near the number of delegates required for nomination. At the convention they ran one-two – Clark/Wilson – for the first 29 ballots. On the 30th, Wilson took the lead; reached a majority on the 43rd; and the two-thirds majority, then required for nomination, on the 46th.

Since Wilson won the election, he was a shoo-in for renomination four years later, but the Democrats threw another whopper of a convention in 1920, with twenty-four different candidates receiving first ballot votes. The real contest came down to former treasury secretary William McAdoo, Wilson's son-in-law whom the president did not endorse; Attorney General A. Mitchell Palmer, remembered for the eponymous post-World War I red-scare raids; New York Governor and future nominee Al Smith; and Ohio Governor James Cox. Cox, who is probably the least remembered of the foursome, won the nomination on the 44th ballot.

But for drama – and no doubt tedium as well – nothing could match the seventeen-day 1924 Democratic Convention. McAdoo, now a Senator from California; and Al Smith contended again, but the nomination went to another candidate that few remember: John Davis, Ambassador to the United Kingdom and former West Virginia Congressman. Davis appears to have been the political Seabiscuit of his day, trailing behind his better-remembered competition for the first ninety-nine rounds before moving up to second place on the 100th ballot and winning on the 103rd.

Conventions tightened up considerably after that, however. On the Democratic side, only two subsequent nominees have required more than a single ballot – FDR, who didn't prevail until a fourth ballot in 1932, due to the two-thirds requirement, and Adlai Stevenson in 1952.

Today's nomination process has become so orderly that someone not paying a lot of attention to politics might be surprised to learn that such a thing as a second ballot would even be possible at a convention, much less a 103rd ballot. Given recent history, most voters would have little cause to think that the process differs

The Democratic Nominating Convention

or could differ in any significant way from any other American electoral process. The delegates convene; a vote is held; a candidate is nominated – or at least that's the way it's been for over sixty years. And with this fading public perception of the particulars of the nominating process we have arrived at a situation today where, when most people vote in a presidential primary, they're simply not entertaining the possibility that there could be any value in voting for someone whom they don't believe can actually win the nomination. An understandable blind spot under these circumstances, certainly, but a crippling one so far as the possibility of long range political change goes.

So, at this juncture, we must reiterate that even though it has fallen into disuse, it is precisely this potential "additive" aspect of the nomination process, allowing for multiple ballots at a convention, that distinguishes the primary (and caucus) process from the final presidential election, and from most other American elections as well. It is precisely this "additive" potential that endows the primaries with the potential to address the "Is best the enemy of better?" dilemma that has historically thwarted the formation of any consistent American electoral left. The essential operative difference here is the majority vote required to win a presidential nomination, in distinction to the simple plurality required to win the Electoral College votes needed to actually be elected president at the end of the process. Or in more identifiably real world terms, the primaries come without the fear that the chance of voting for the really good choices comes only at the expense of hurting the chances of the not-necessarily-always-all-that-good-but-generally-reliably-better-than-the-Republican options in the usual "subtractive" American electoral process.

The achievements of the 2004 Kucinich presidential campaign were modest at best, and those of 2008 more modest yet. But that shouldn't prevent us from learning from it. At the time, it was a widely accepted that Kucinich would, and actually did, get far fewer votes than there were voters who actually agreed with him. Otherwise Kucinich could reasonably have expected primary votes on the order of the numbers recorded by Jesse Jackson sixteen years earlier. Kucinich, after all, was reviving some of the Jackson campaign's concerns more audibly than any other Democratic presidential primary contender had since then and

The Primary Route

there was no reason to think that the constituency for those ideas had gone away.

Obviously most of the huge difference in their vote totals stems from the fact that Kucinich had no reach into Jackson's broad base of African-American support. But there was more – there were millions of voters on the left who never looked past Howard Dean in 2004 or John Edwards in 2008 because conventional wisdom had it that Dean and Edwards were the left-most of the candidates who were "viable." And again, given that most voters were not alive the last time a nominee had been forced to seek another candidate's supporters at a convention, their quick take on the situation seemed to make perfect sense. To further cloud matters, the other primaries on the ballot the very same day as the presidential primaries generally operate in the "subtractive," plurality-winner-take-all basis common to most American elections. Relatively few voters were likely to even consider the possibility that they actually might have a better opportunity to vote for what they *really* wanted in the presidential race than in congressional primary taking place on the same day, on the same ballot.

The simple fact is that in 2004 and 2008 there just weren't a lot of voters going to the polls who could conceive of any kind of scenario where delegates they sent to a convention committed to a candidate they really liked might ultimately play a role in steering the nomination to a candidate who might have been their second or third choice, rather than one who might have been, say, their fourth or fifth choice. And yet the fact is that if we want to do the hard analysis of what political course of action makes the most sense in our actual political system, it is precisely this aspect of the system that we need to comprehend and eventually to utilize.[35]

Now, to be fair to the voters, we might also argue that Kucinich himself didn't do everything he might have to encourage that kind of "back to the future" thinking, either. Kucinich, who was first elected to the Cleveland, Ohio City Council at age 23 and as mayor at 31, won a war with the local economic power structure when he refused to sell the city's publicly owned electric utility, only to lose his subsequent battle for reelection.[36] Neither his

The Democratic Nominating Convention

personal story nor his look bore the mark of approval of central political candidate casting. He was treated dismissively by the powers that be in all of the ways those who would challenge the status quo usually are. All of this added up to the fact that he was rather unlikely to actually ever win the nomination. The situation might have called for him to try to break the "fourth wall" of the presidential primary process and introduce the idea that he didn't actually have to have a chance at winning the nomination for his campaign to be valuable. Taking the case *against* the Iraq War and *for* a Canadian-style "single payer" health care system and *for* major military budget cuts as far as possible in that year's presidential campaign would have been reason enough to justify his effort. But then no one had made that argument in a really long time and such an acknowledgment might only have made it even easier for establishment institutions to dismiss him. Where Jackson had a substantial base that supported that type of insight into the process intuitively, Kucinich did not.

Most assuredly, the idea of positively impacting a national political convention via a candidacy that falls short of ultimately winning the nomination flies in the face of a seemingly inexorable trend of conventions becoming ever more tightly scripted affairs designed to show the world a thoroughly unified party. But then the process of mastering the mechanics of our presidential election process is probably relatively child's play compared with the broader goals of challenging and ultimately altering our destructive (and self-destructive) militarist foreign policy and our out-of-control capitalist system, if indeed we are serious about this.

Of course, to revert to rock hard contemporary fact, as previously noted, it is the case that right now most of the guardians of allowable political discourse would cast the very idea of a convention that required more than one ballot to choose a nominee as a dangerous and divisive display of disunity. And there is arguably some truth to the Obama campaign's perception that a Clinton campaign continuing all the way to the election might have been damaging in the sense that the Obama-Clinton race was only rarely about issues and mostly constituted an argument about which of the two possessed the superior leadership characteristics, a situation lending itself to negative campaigning more than a difference on the issues might.

131

The Primary Route

It may be too much to expect our presidential candidates for the near future to invoke the possibility of the reappearance of the multi-ballot convention, given all of the difficulty they will encounter in simply conveying the actual issues that make them run. But what we absolutely do need is candidates committed to shifting the discussion toward those issues and ideas and away from the candidates' personalities, and even their supposed *abilities*. It's not a matter of the identity of the candidate becoming insignificant – some messengers will always prove a lot more successful at delivering their message than others. But if we are to see any kind of breakthrough campaigns in the future, they will require, at the least, candidates more movement-oriented than career-oriented, who argue more for *what* they think needs to be done rather than *who* needs to do it or why they are *the one* to do it. More *we* candidacies and fewer *me* candidacies. And rather than making the nomination process more divisive, we might actually envision candidacies of this nature ideally contributing to a more civilized atmosphere of debate, which is precisely what will we need if we want to imagine the backers of disparate candidates unifying once the nominating process is over. Agreeing to disagree is a lot easier, and more rational, than backing someone you've argued just didn't have what it takes to serve in the White House.

This book is hardly intended as a manual for candidates, though. Rather it is primarily a plea to the voter: The best candidates imaginable can do little if there aren't voters out there with their ears trained to hear them. If we're ever hoping for a presidential candidacy that can transform the national political debate, with the tenacity to run wire to wire – first caucuses to last primaries, all the way through the convention – then *we* have to be voters who are ready to recognize those campaigns and willing to vote for them, support them and even seek them out.

We don't have to think that our candidate is likely to win the nomination to make the effort of a candidacy of the left worthwhile. Nor do we even have to assume that we will be able to bring the convention's additive potential back into the picture right away by keeping a less-than-ideal front-runner from wrapping it up before the convention. But if we can simply imagine a champion of the common people taking an anti-elitist

The Democratic Nominating Convention

economic program from the first presidential primary debate all the way through the last and onto the convention, then we have envisioned the potential of a serious candidacy of the left. And if we can imagine continuing to address the big audience each time out, change on the national level will follow.

And in the Mean Time - the Platform

Given how long a time has passed since the last multiple-ballot convention, we can't count on another one happening real soon. And it could also prove to be awhile before a candidate of the left, as loosely defined in this book, wins the nomination outright. These probabilities need not automatically leave delegates of the left with nothing to do at nominating conventions, however. The party also adopts a platform. While the platform has been dramatically de-emphasized in recent years, it has in the past been considered worth talking about, sometimes even worth fighting about. On the face of it, it only seems logical that the question of what a party claims to stand for should be seen as a matter of some significance. And if we hope to actually influence the course of the national political debate, we certainly need to consider whether it might be worthwhile to take up the fight about the content of party platforms once again.

After he won the 1996 Republican presidential nomination, a reporter asked the famously sarcastic Robert Dole whether he would follow his party's platform. The candidate replied, "I don't know. I haven't read it." While no recent Democratic nominee has quite matched Dole's dismissiveness, it seems likely that little more than a modicum of politeness distinguishes the attitude of today's candidates of both parties from that of the former Senator from Kansas. The increasingly entrepreneurial nature of the modern presidential candidacy seems by its nature to imply diminished attention to a platform that might actually reflect the views of others outside of that candidate's inner circle. To a greater and greater extent each time around, it seems, a major party's presidential campaign politics are what its candidate says they are. This is not to say that the candidates aren't being told what positions to take, it's just that the people telling them aren't going to be elected party delegates.

The Platform

Women's suffrage occasioned the Democrats' first big twentieth century platform fight in 1916.

A party platform that might say anything different is increasingly viewed as a potential hindrance to election, and little more.

For those of us looking to broaden the scope of the national presidential debate to more fundamental discussions of war and peace, wealth and poverty, democracy and power, however, it's an entirely different matter. What better opportunity are we ever presented to separate the facts out from the personalities than in the making of a party platform?

The draft platform is adopted by a platform committee that meets in advance of the convention itself. Democratic Party Platform Committee members are chosen by the same proportional methods as are the actual delegates. A candidate winning fifteen percent of a convention's delegates will also get fifteen percent of the platform committee, although platform committee members needn't actually be convention delegates. Current rules require that in order for a minority report to be brought before the entire convention, it must have gained the support of twenty percent of the platform committee membership. And as past presidential conventions have demonstrated, losing at the committee level

The Primary Route

doesn't necessarily doom a proposal to defeat at the convention. In some cases, a loser in committee may even go on to become a history-making proposition!

The first particularly significant platform fight of the early modern days of presidential campaigning came over the woman's suffrage question in 1916. The Democratic Platform Committee majority report simply called for extending the right vote to women, while the minority report called for leaving the matter up to the individual states to decide, which was essentially the Republican position. In that convention's only platform floor fight, the minority plank was resoundingly rejected by a 888 ½-181 ½ vote and, as it turned out, the fact that the proponents of the minority position chose to take their fight before the entire convention probably benefitted the Democrats by highlighting their differences with the Republicans on the issue.[37]

The Klanbake

With its 103 ballots, the 1924 New York Democratic Convention was one for the ages. And it didn't lack for hot platform debate either. By 742 ½ to 353 ½, delegates backed a majority report that called for a national referendum on the question of whether the U.S. should join the League of Nations and the World Court. Since the defeated minority plank simply called for the U.S. to join the organization without qualification, the majority report, and the convention's ultimate stance, represented a rebuke of Woodrow Wilson, the most recent Democratic president, who had championed the new organizations. And so far as the mechanisms of government go, the majority plank was also actually quite radical, in that the United States had never before, and has never since, conducted a national referendum on anything.

But this was not even the really hot issue of that convention. That distinction went to the question of whether the Democrats would denounce the Ku Klux Klan by name. At one point 20,000 Klan supporters gathered across the river in New Jersey in opposition to that effort. The hubbub caused newspapers to dub the convention the "Klanbake." Ultimately, the minority report which opposed *"any effort on the part of the Ku Klux Klan or any*

The Platform

The Ku Klux Klan, shown relaxing here, were the big issue in 1924.

organization to interfere with the religious liberty or political freedom of any citizen, or to limit the civic rights of any citizen or body of citizens because of religion, birth place, or racial origin" failed by the narrowest margin ever recorded at Democratic convention, 543 7/20 to 543 3/20, or one fifth of a vote. Progressive Party presidential candidate Robert La Follette subsequently denounced the Klan on the campaign trail and Democratic nominee John Davis ultimately did so as well. Given that the former states of the Confederacy had become the "Solid South" of the Democratic Party, the level of anti-Klan sentiment that did exist within the party is actually quite striking, particularly in contrast to the situation within the Republican Party where not only did Republican incumbent Calvin Coolidge decline to condemn the Klan, but proponents of doing so could not even muster enough support to bring a similar anti-Klan resolution to the floor of the party convention.

There are also other aspects of past Democratic Party platforms that did not even require a major fight, yet stand out as noteworthy today. The 1932 platform, for instance, stated that, *"We condemn the improper and excessive use of money in political activities. We condemn paid lobbies of special interests to influence members of Congress and other public servants by personal contact."* It's hard to imagine getting something like that in a platform today, at least not without a major floor fight.

Walking in Sunshine

The 1916 and 1924 platform fights are largely forgotten today, but one from the 1948 convention has continued to reverberate on into twenty-first century memory. In many ways a continuation of the debate twenty-four years earlier, the most controversial platform issue at the 1948 convention was the party's potential civil rights plank. Arguing on behalf of the minority report, Hubert Humphrey, then mayor of Minneapolis and candidate for U.S. Senator from Minnesota, memorably argued that the Democrats needed to "get out of the shadow of states' rights and walk forthrightly into the bright sunshine of human rights." It's estimated that sixty million people heard this speech on the radio, while an additional ten million more watched it on television.[38]

The matter of contention was the final paragraph of the minority report:

We call upon the Congress to support our President in guaranteeing these basic and fundamental American Principles:
(1) the right of full and equal political participation;
(2) the right to equal opportunity of employment;

The Platform

(3) the right of security of person and
(4) the right of equal treatment in the service and defense of our nation.

Half the nation heard Hubert Humphrey tell the 1948 Democrats to "get out of the shadow of states' rights."

While the content of this amendment did not in itself pose a substantive problem for President Harry Truman, he had hoped to placate southern delegates by keeping the specific language out of the platform. But that was not to be, as the convention adopted the minority report by a 651 ½ to 582 ½ margin. As Truman had feared, the issue actually split the Democratic Party, with three dozen southern delegates responding to the convention vote by walking out, thereby beginning a process that would result in the creation of the States' Rights Party, or "Dixiecrats," which ran South Carolina Governor Strom Thurmond for president.   Not only was this the most stunning victory for a minority report at a

The Primary Route

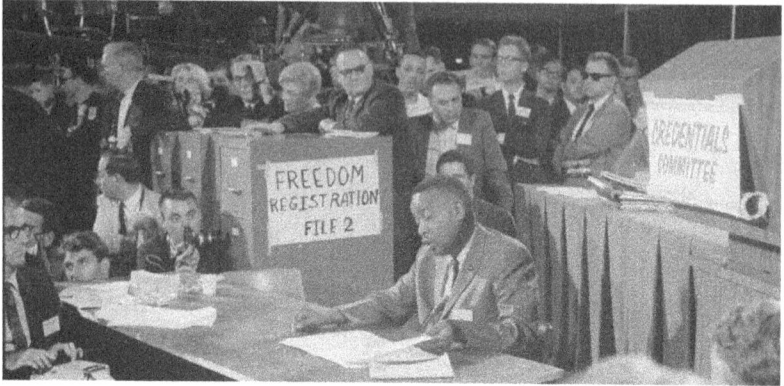

The Mississippi Freedom Democratic Party asserted its right to replace the state's 1964 official delegation.

modern Democratic convention, but it arguably also stands as the important platform debate held within the party in the modern era. The impact of that floor fight would continue to be felt for decades, in that this dispute may be seen as the beginning of an historic process of national political realignment, triggering a profound shift in loyalty within America's black population away from the party of Abraham Lincoln and toward the Democrats, accompanied by a shift in the opposite direction on the part of Southern whites. Truman's upset win that November was probably crucial to the way it all played out subsequently: had he not won, we can easily envision a scenario in which the party's bold-for-its-time embrace of civil rights would have been blamed for a defeat at the polls and the issue would be considered "too hot to handle" for years to come.   In 1960, the party's civil rights plank again proved to be the greatest source of convention controversy, as North Carolina Senator Sam Ervin, of later Watergate Hearing fame, introduced motions to delete several of the draft platform's stated goals. Ervin opposed the proposals to make the Civil Rights Commission a permanent agency, to grant the attorney general the power to file civil injunction suits to prevent discrimination, and to set 1963 as the deadline for the initiation of school desegregation plans. All of Ervin's motions, however, lost on voice votes.

The Platform

And in 1964, in the midst of what we now think of as the Civil Rights Era, yet another civil rights question emerged as the convention's most contentious issue. This time, however, the dispute came from the credentials committee rather than the platform committee. The specific question at hand was who would represent Mississippi – the all-white delegation actually chosen in the primary or the racially integrated group sent by the Mississippi Freedom Democratic Party in protest of the state's laws that prevented blacks from registering to vote. The dispute resulted in a compromise which was not acceptable to all parties. The convention seated the official delegation, offered two at-large seats to the Freedom Democrats, and committed future conventions to barring delegations chosen under discriminatory procedures such as those in place in Mississippi when this current delegation had been selected.

Stop the Bombing

The 1968 Chicago Democratic Convention easily matched any other convention of the twentieth century in terms of crowd fervor, both in the convention hall and in the streets. Only one platform committee debate reached the convention floor, but it was the one that concerned what the shouting was all about – the party's stance on the Vietnam War, the other major issue of what popular history generally remembers as "the 60s."

Prior to the Platform Committee meeting, antiwar presidential candidate Minnesota Senator Gene McCarthy offered a Vietnam plank that called for an unconditional halt to U.S. bombing of North Vietnam, general de-escalation of the war and the creation of a South Vietnam coalition government that included the participation of the National Liberation Front, the pro-unification enemy of the Saigon government that the U.S. had been supporting. The proposal stated that, *"If the present leaders of South Vietnam refuse to agree to such a broadly based coalition, we will then withdraw our support and our forces since an honorable peace will no longer be possible."* A later compromise proposal, described by one of its backers as

The Primary Route

In 1968, the issue was the Vietnam War.

"deliberately mild," but insistent on the point of the unconditional bombing halt, was offered by backers of McCarthy and McGovern. It read:

"That war must be ended now. It will not be ended by a military victory, surrender, or unilateral withdrawal by either side; it cannot be ended by further United States escalation, either increasing our troops, introducing nuclear weapons, or extending the conflict geographically: it must therefore be ended by a fair and realistic compromise settlement ...

"We will then negotiate a mutual withdrawal of all United States forces and all North Vietnamese forces from South Vietnam. This should be a phased withdrawal over a relatively short period of time ...

"The South Vietnamese will assume increasing responsibility for the resolution of the conflict, and full responsibility for determining their own political destiny ...

The Platform

"We will lower the level of violence by reducing offensive operations in the Vietnamese countryside, thus enabling an early withdrawal of a significant number of our troops.

"In this way we can eliminate all foreign forces from South Vietnam. Our troops will leave and those of North Vietnam will also depart. It will be up to the South Vietnamese to achieve a political and social reconciliation of their warring peoples."

The bottom line in this dispute was that an unconditional bombing halt was unacceptable to sitting Democratic President Lyndon Johnson. The president went so far as to bring General William Westmoreland, commander of all U.S. forces in Vietnam, to a White House meeting to tell Senate members of the platform committee that, "A bombing halt would endanger the lives of American troops." Johnson himself told them, "If the bombing were stopped, the enemy's capacity in the DMZ [the demilitarized zone between North and South Vietnam] would increase by 500 percent."

Despite the widespread understanding that it was precisely the unpopularity of his war policy that prevented Johnson from standing for reelection, Vice President and nominee-in-the-making Hubert Humphrey went along with the administration program. As a result, the Vietnam plank that emerged from the platform committee read, *"Stop all bombing of North Vietnam when this action would not endanger the lives of our troops in the field. This action should take into account the response from Hanoi."*

After two days of debate at the convention, that position prevailed by a 1, 567 ¾ to 1,041 ¼. Although the outcome was a foregone conclusion, the impact of this vote – which appeared to commit the country to at least four more years of war – was dramatic and far-reaching. Not only would it affect the election that November, but this division would be felt for decades within the Democratic Party – and some might even argue that the ripples from that split remain visible today.

The Primary Route

The McGovern Platform

In some respects the 1972 Democratic Platform stands alone. The fact that no less than twenty different minority planks would actually come to the floor of that convention, with two winning, speaks to the level of free wheeling within the party at that moment. But more remarkable still was the actual document that the majority passed – in both the platform committee and the convention as a whole. Just as George McGovern was arguably the most left wing candidate to win the Democratic Party presidential nomination in the modern era, the 1972 platform he ran on was arguably also the most left wing document of its kind.

Opening with the statement that *"Skepticism and cynicism are widespread in America,"* the document averred that the American people now *"feel that the government is run for the privileged few rather than for the many-and they are right."* So far as the central question of the Vietnam War went, it proposed to *"end that war by a simple plan that need not be kept secret: The immediate total withdrawal of all Americans from Southeast Asia."*

At the same time, while many of the 1972 platform themes might seem extraordinary were they to appear in a twenty-first century platform, some of them were actually quite consistent with Democratic platforms from the surrounding years. For instance, in putting the party on record as *"committed to a job for every American who seeks work"* and *"determined to make economic security a matter of right,"* the McGovern platform was consistent with previous platforms referring to a commitment to "full employment." At the same time, the 1972 language addressed the issue in probably the most explicit terms ever found in a policy document emanating from a major party convention: *"Full employment—a guaranteed job for all—is the primary economic objective of the Democratic Party."* And lest any ambiguity remain, it stated, *"This means a job with decent pay and good working conditions for everyone willing and able to work and an adequate income for those unable to work."*

The platform also committed to *"Closing tax loopholes that encourage the export of American jobs by American-controlled multi-national corporations,"* deplored *"the increasing*

The Platform

concentration of economic power in fewer and fewer hands," and concluded that *"The Democratic Administration should pledge itself to combat factors which tend to concentrate wealth and stimulate higher prices"* and *"deconcentrate shared monopolies such as auto, steel and tire industries which administer prices, create unemployment through restricted output and stifle technological innovation."* And then there was a pledge to *"Stiffen the civil and criminal statutes to make corporate officers responsible for their actions,"* to boot.

A few conventions down the road, Gary Hart, at the time a U.S. Senator from Colorado, McGovern's 1972 campaign manager, and a principal contender for the presidential nomination, would break what was then considered new ground ideologically, in that while he was generally considered to be on the party's "liberal" wing, he counted unions among the "special interests" that his candidacy set out to challenge.

The view in 1972 was radically different, as the party platform declared that "Through their great trade union organizations, these men and women, have exerted tremendous influence on the economic and social life of the nation and have attained a standard of living known to no other nation. The concern of the Party is that the gains which labor struggled so long to obtain not be lost to them, whether through inaction or subservience to illogical Republican domestic policies." Pledging "continued support for our system of free collective bargaining" and denouncing "any attempt to substitute compulsory arbitration for it," the platform advocated "collective bargaining rights for government employees" (as the 1968 platform had also done), "universal coverage and longer duration of the Unemployment Insurance and Workmen's Compensation programs," as well as expanding minimum wage coverage to "the 16 million workers not presently covered, including domestic workers, service workers, agricultural employees and employees of governmental and nonprofit agencies."

Yet, as we know, the AFL-CIO chose not to back George McGovern's candidacy, despite the fact that he was running on platform whose commitment to the American working class was unmatched in the past century. The degree to which Gary Hart's

145

The Primary Route

subsequent reassessment of unions derived from the AFL-CIO's stance in 1972 is unclear. What is indisputable, however, is that the share of the American workforce belonging to unions, which had been over a third for much of the forties and fifties, has dropped from about a quarter in 1972 to less than half of that today, its lowest level in almost a century. And while there have obviously been other more important factors in that decline, it is also true that the AFL-CIO's failure to line up on the same side of the burning question of the day, alongside those who wished to be its allies, seriously damaged the organization's reputation in many places it ought to have cared about. And nowhere did it fail in this regard more infamously than in its snub of McGovern.

The 1972 platform also marked the apex of the Democratic Party's health care reform ambitions, envisioning a *"universal National Health Insurance"* that would be *"federally-financed and federally-administered,"* covering *"all Americans with a comprehensive set of benefits including preventive medicine, mental and emotional disorders, and complete protection against catastrophic costs,"* with *"the rule of free choice for both provider and consumer ... protected,"* and *"incentives and controls to curb inflation in health care costs and to assure efficient delivery of all services."* And the 1972 platform's section denouncing the Nixon Administration's *"epidemic of wiretapping and electronic surveillance"* also now seems eerily resonant.

Of course, not everything in the platform represented a victory for the left. The George Wallace campaign's minority planks on guns, school prayer, the death penalty and school busing all failed, but so did proposals from the left advocating a guaranteed annual income and the Harris tax reform. Also losing were positions we have now come to take for granted concerning reproductive rights and gay rights. And the Israel plank – one of the two minority reports adopted – made no mention of Palestinians; the word "Palestinian" would not appear in a platform committee document until 1980.

The two subsequent conventions were quite disparate in demeanor – 1976 saw only a single minority report come to the floor, while 1980 had two days of roll calls and 17 hours of debate.

The Platform

Yet the actual platforms that came out of the two conventions were not terribly different – and on some issues both were far more similar to 1972's than to anything we'd find in the most recent platforms. The 1976 program affirmed *"the right of all adult Americans willing, able and seeking work to have opportunities for useful jobs at living wages,"* while 1980's specified *"commitment to achieve all the goals of the Humphrey-Hawkins Full Employment Act."* (The Humphrey-Hawkins bill – signed into law by President Carter in 1978 – directed the government to achieve an overall unemployment rate no higher than 4 percent and an adult rate no higher than 3 percent and established the right of the government to serve as the employer of last resort should the private sector prove unable and/or unwilling to meet these goals. Its goals were largely unmet and the law has since expired.)

The 1976 platform also backed *"a comprehensive national health insurance system with universal and mandatory coverage"* that *"should be financed by a combination of employer-employee shared payroll taxes and general tax revenues."* 1980's document more generally supported *"a comprehensive, universal national health insurance plan."* Both conventions continued to support collective bargaining rights for public employees and agricultural workers, although support for expanding minimum wage coverage disappeared.

Four years of the Reagan presidency brought a new dynamic to the 1984 Democratic Convention, as many mainstream Democrats tacked right but an electoral left also reappeared. The early stirrings of the left first manifested themselves in a truncated and now largely forgotten run by 1972 nominee George McGovern. Better remembered, however, was Jesse Jackson's first candidacy. The Jackson campaign brought four minority planks to the convention floor, including the first foreign policy challenges since 1972: An amendment eschewing first use of nuclear weapons lost by a 56.3 to 35.7% margin and a call for reduced defense spending failed by 65.9 to 28.7%. A *"commitment to full employment"* survived in the party platform; however, national health insurance did not.

Following an expanded Jackson campaign, the 1988 convention exhibited a similar dynamic: The no-first-nuclear-

The Primary Route

weapons-use plank lost by a larger margin this time – 59.5 to 29.3%. A Jackson "fair tax" plank fared even worse, failing by 60 to 26.2%. But a commitment to a *"first-rate full employment economy"* did make it through one more platform committee cut. By 1992, all discussion of "full employment" would disappear from the party platform (it has yet to reappear) and the only platform challenge to the Clinton campaign came from the right, as the Paul Tsongas campaign's "middle class tax cut" lost 2287 to 953.

In 2000, a proposed Medicare expansion did make the platform with the argument that *"Americans aged 55 to 65 ... should be allowed to buy into the Medicare program."* This was not reiterated in 2004.

While little in the 2008 platform was new, the Obama campaign treated its development as an organizing opportunity. The final document cites over fifteen hundred public hearings and meetings in all fifty states that took place as part of the process of the document's creation. It foresaw *"a wide array of health insurance plans, including many private health insurance options and a public plan"* and further argued that *"families should have health insurance coverage similar to what Members of Congress enjoy."*

By 2012, the platform's discussion of health insurance was largely devoted to an appreciation of the merits of the Affordable Care Act, the Obama Administration's signal legislative achievement. And so far as controversy went, the administration itself was the source of the only floor actions, as a decision was made to reassert – via floor amendment – that Americans' *"potential"* is *"God-given"* and that *"Jerusalem is and will remain the capital of Israel."* This language had been in the 2008 platform but was not in the 2012 platform committee document and now it turned out that where the Republican platform had referred to the Supreme Being a dozen times, the Democrats' committee draft was making no mention of "God" at all. The floor amendment was designed to address this imbalance. (The number of "no"s audible during the full convention vote on naming the capital of Israel was sufficient to cause the chair to call the question three times; no roll

The Platform

call was ordered.)

And so it is that the twenty-first century has yet to experience its first substantive Democratic convention political debate.

The Primaries (and Caucuses) – How Do We Do It?

If it's true that we "government of the people" sorts have only rarely taken advantage of the potential of the presidential primary system, we can plead the excuse that we often simply didn't really recognize it for what it was. In the midst of the widely disparate systems of elections in use in these United States, maybe we simply failed to appreciate the particulars of the primary system. It did, after all, take the better part of a century for the primaries to become as central to the presidential election process as they have now become, so you might say we kind of never noticed the primary tree as it was growing up in the midst of the lush forest of American electoral variants. So far as the diversity of the American electoral system goes, the 2000 Bush-Gore election was a real eye-opener for a lot of the nation. The Florida ballot recount process provided millions with their first good look at the complexity to be found in the nitty gritty of American elections. First off, anyone who had not been paying attention back in social studies class the day they told you about the Electoral College got a quick real-life refresher as, for the first time since Benjamin Harrison took it from Grover Cleveland in 1888, we watched the presidency go to a candidate who indisputably did not receive the highest number of actual popular votes.

The question of who got the most votes in Florida, on the other hand, was highly disputed. And the recounts that ensued provided a remarkable display of just how widely the specific procedures through which American elections are conducted could vary – and not just from state to state, but even from one county to the next. Not only are there the 50 states and the District of Columbia setting election laws, but there are 3,007 counties and 137 county equivalents in the United States. And probably

The Primaries and Caucuses

unbeknownst to most people, not only may these counties establish their own electoral structures, as do cities and towns, but most also have the power to determine the actual specific methods of voting and vote counting for all of the elections within their jurisdictions. So not only may you vote for different types of offices from one city or county to the next, e.g., city council, board of supervisors, etc., but two different parts of the same state may use different methods to vote in elections for same state and federal offices.

Voters in most of these counties would have been totally unfamiliar with the subtleties of "hanging chads" that suddenly loomed so important in Florida because their own local voting system worked in an entirely different manner. Some of them voted with paper ballots, but in a tremendous variety of methods. Some voted on one of any number of different voting machines. Some of their ballots were counted by hand and some by machine. And increasingly they voted by mail. In Oregon everyone votes by mail. In America, who's got time to think through the implications of the presidential primary process when you're busy trying to figure out how "butterfly ballots" work?

But when we ever do get down to the details of the primary system, we find it holds a double advantage. Fundamentally, it is the "subtractive" aspect of the American presidential election that compels us to make our political stand first in the primaries. The electoral college vote that actually elects the president is a simple state by state, plurality-winner-takes-all system, which is also the method determining the winner for most other American elections. With there generally being no way possible to combine two or more candidates' or parties' votes, our system has a devastating effect upon "third parties," by putting would-be third party voters in the position of effectively subtracting from the chances of the party that their preferred candidate would most likely ally with, if our system offered a way to add the votes of two parties. This structure has marginalized third parties into a protest role for a very long time – and seems likely to continue to do so for the foreseeable future.

This factor in itself would demand a strategy of working in the primaries, even if the primaries themselves also embodied this same "subtractive," plurality-winner-takes-all problem. But they don't. In the primaries it takes only 15% of the vote from a single congressional district for a presidential candidate to get on the delegate scoreboard. And from there, although it has been largely unutilized in recent years, elected delegates have the power to combine with delegates who were elected in support of like-minded candidates – the rare example of an "additive" aspect in the American electoral system.

Has any campaign actually worked out anything like this in a really long time? Absolutely not, but then, if one had, we wouldn't need to be having this discussion in the first place. The argument in this book is not that the primary route to mainstream relevance for the American left would be easy, only that would be *possible,* unlike some other options.

Should we start to get wise to the opportunities inherent in the primaries, we can be sure that established interests of great wealth and power will come to the fore to make our efforts unwelcome. On the conceptual level, the argument will be made that the more intense the ideological gauntlet we force the presidential candidates to run in the nominating process, the more we threaten the viability of the ultimate nominee in the final election. Implicit in this is the argument that we will be better off simply accepting the candidates that recognized "opinion leaders" present us with. And as for the part about the rival candidates' delegates potentially joining forces at a convention based upon the issues, or even just the idea of a second ballot, fuggedaboudit, that sort of thing is just not done any more. TV time is already booked.

The dangers of conducting too fractious a debate during the nominating campaign are real and cannot be dismissed categorically. Any real political campaign involves not only the possibility of failure, but the danger of inadvertently making things worse. Action involves risk. And there will never be any one-fits-all-situations answer to the question of how to best approach a particular campaign. Politics is a lot messier than ideology and theory for the simple reason that it involves actual people and actual people disagree, with great frequency. And if you carry the argument for caution through to its logical conclusion, the way to minimize the potential for a debate becoming too divisive is simply to have no debate at all. For supporters of the status quo, there really would be little upside to engaging in the sort of presidential primary activity this book advocates.

Those of us on the other side of that divide, on the other hand, need to pose ourselves the question continually of how we can hope to ever *make* big change without first finding a way to *talk about* big change, not just on our blogs or in our newsletters, but to the millions of people who may not have politics first thing on their minds when they get up every morning.

Candidates unfortunately come with no guarantees. Even when they are excellent on the issues it does not necessarily follow that they will be gifted campaigners. Can we find candidates able to respectfully beg to differ with the opposition on the issues? Do we have a candidate who meets the perceived seriousness hurdle? Does this particular candidate argue effectively? Will that one inevitably be smeared out of viability? Would more than one candidate of the left be okay, or would this destroy the prospects of both (or more) candidates? We have to make decisions like this each time around, like it or not.

Over the years, we on the American left have become very used to taking our electoral system to task for its failings so far as not providing equal opportunity for the interests of those who are not rich and powerful, and this with good cause. But committing to serious engagement in the presidential nomination process may mean that in the future we spend less time making that critique at arm's length and more time within the current system, maximizing such opportunities as it actually *does* provide.

Learning the Rules

As giant a step as it would be for the American left to even to make the decision to *try* to become serious players in national politics, it would only be the first step of many. Before we even find the candidates, we have to learn the rules. In 2008, the last year that the nomination was in doubt, Democratic primaries were held in 36 states plus the District of Columbia and caucuses convened in the other 14 states. And although residents of Puerto Rico, American Samoa, Guam and the U.S. Virgin Islands are unable to actually vote for the president of the United States, they can participate in choosing the Democratic Party's nominee. To that end, Puerto Rico held a primary, while the other three territories chose delegates in caucuses. Additionally there was a primary for Democrats Abroad. And as is the case with the actual elections, when it comes to the delegate selection process, one cannot assume that understanding the process in one state means understanding the process in them all.

Currently 81% of the total number of Democratic convention delegates are selected in primaries and caucuses. While Republican Party rules still allow for winner-take-all primaries, all state Democratic parties are required to allocate delegates proportionally among all candidates receiving at least 15% of the vote in a particular congressional district. But beyond this, the rules vary tremendously from state to state. Some hold "open" primaries, allowing any registered voter to participate, regardless of party registration. Some hold "closed" primaries, allowing only Democrats to vote. Some hold "semi-closed" primaries, open to Democrats and independents. Some allow non-Democrats to vote, on the condition that they change their registration to Democrat. Each of these situations may call for somewhat different approach. There are 56 separate contests choosing delegates, with 56 sets of rules and a full-blown presidential campaign has to master them all.[39]

How Do We Proceed?

As if to discourage us from thinking that we ever really understand the presidential nominating process, the fact is that although primaries determine the selection of the vast majority of the delegates chosen by the voters, 87% in 2008, the first presidential convention delegate contest each time around is not a primary, but a series of caucuses, a method, used mostly in smaller states, that represents something of a throwback to the systems in place in the days before primaries became dominant.

The Iowa Caucuses are traditionally held in January or February, shortly before the New Hampshire Primary. Since they require not only that you show up to vote, with no vote-by-mail

The Primaries and Caucuses

option, but that you stick around for a few hours, they draw a more committed level of voter. In 2008 – the last year there was a serious contest – the Iowa Democratic caucuses drew about 235,000 participants to 1,774 separate precinct meetings. Although this represented a dramatic increase in participation from previous years, the number still represented only about 28.5% of the total number that would vote for Obama in the state in November. By way of comparison, the overall nationwide number of Democratic primary and caucus voters was about 53.8% of the Democratic vote in the final election. So we might argue that the average Iowa caucus-goer is nearly twice as motivated as the average primary voter, or conversely that a caucus-goer is about twice as hard to come by as a primary voter.

What is for certain, though, is that Iowa caucus voters have direct experience with the type of "additive" rules that facilitate coalition building and that can operate in the presidential nominating convention, where they have largely fallen into disuse. The same 15% percent rule applies in the Iowa Democratic caucuses as applies in Democratic primary votes, but whereas in primary states this means that a candidate must get at least 15% of a congressional district's vote in order to share in that district's allotted number of delegates, in Iowa the 15% rule extends all the way down to the precinct caucus level. And with such a large number of separate meetings, there will be many instances in which particular candidates will have less than 15% support in a caucus, forcing their backers to decide whether to join forces with the supporters of their second or third choice candidates. In some cases these decisions will be made ad hoc, according to the preferences of the individual voters. In others, a campaign may advise its people to coalesce with the supporters of one particular rival candidate, based upon perceived political similarities or other strategic campaign concerns. In Iowa, at least, tactical voting is a practical reality. Iowa voters have reason to understand that supporting a candidate who may not ultimately win the nomination is part of the process, not a waste of their vote.

The Primary Route

Well, Iowa's One Thing, but the Nation?

Iowa affords us the best known real life example of presidential electoral coalition politics. While it's true that there hasn't been a presidential nomination second ballot since 1952 (or a second ballot of any kind since the 1956 Democratic vice-presidential nomination), the fact remains that there could be a second ballot. And it is that simple fact that gives the presidential nominating process – and the primaries and caucuses that are a part of it – the potential to break the political logjam in which the American left has been mired for decade after decade. If we are looking to expand the bounds of American politics to allow people the opportunity to vote for what they hope to see happen and not merely against what they fear may happen, if we are looking for the place to run candidates who are willing to say what needs to be said, rather than just estimating what will bring them immediate success, then the primaries and caucuses are where we need to be. And Iowa shows how it works. The state, in a sense, represents the overall process writ small.

Primary state voters are considerably less likely than caucus-goers to think about tactical voting choices. It is, after all, a lot harder to assess how your preferred candidates are going to fare in your state, or your congressional district, than it is to simply count their supporters standing in front of you at a precinct caucus. Nonetheless, just as British voters over the years developed their own methods of tactical voting within a less than ideal system, we may also need to become more discerning in how we utilize our own system. For instance, if we want to make the most of our opportunities, fully prepared primary voters will probably want to be aware of what situations might warrant a vote for someone other than their first choice. While we can hope that the sorts of candidates we'd like to see in future presidential races will be able to run 50-state+ races, we should be prepared for a reality that might fall short of that ideal. And if our favorite candidate simply isn't a factor in the primary in our own state, or district, we may want to be prepared to switch to the best available candidate with a chance of reaching the 15% hurdle. Just as candidates sometimes direct or request their Iowa supporters to caucus with the supporters of another candidate when their own support is lacking,

The Primaries and Caucuses

we might imagine candidates doing something similar on a nationwide basis. Or we might imagine a collection of favorite sons or daughters of the left, running campaigns confined to the states or regions of their greatest strength. There are, in other words, innumerable ways of approaching the complexities of the American electoral system.

The Primary Route

Counter Arguments

The central argument of this book – that if we seriously mean to develop into a national political force capable of significantly affecting our country's foreign and economic policy we will need to challenge the status quo positions in the presidential election process, specifically in the primaries – has been two-pronged, directed against both the view that third parties are the left's best, most appropriate avenue for presidential politics, and the idea that casting your primary vote for a candidate who might not win the nomination constitutes a waste of that vote. But these are far from the only arguments that are, or might be advanced in opposition to this book's point of view.

You Have to Start Local (or Maybe with Congress)

One argument has it that focusing on developing a left presence in presidential politics has things backward. To really affect things, according to this line of thinking, you've got to start small and build up from the local level – school board, city council, mayor. Another variant has it that our focus should be on statehouses because state governments are the "laboratories of democracy," the places where real innovation starts. And then there are those who agree with a national focus, but think that trying to affect the presidential race is gross overreach and that we should focus on Congress instead.

One thing this book definitely is not is any kind of political "theory of everything." Where it argues that being in the presidential primaries is something we need to do if we ever intend to be a serious political force, it does not claim, or mean to imply, that it constitutes everything that we need to do. There's no contention here that the primaries eclipse all else in importance. There's no expectation that everyone who follows the argument herein immediately drops everything and climbs on the bandwagon. There's not even a presumption that it would be the best thing if they did.

There's no argument intended here that contesting offices on any and all of the lower levels of government is of any less importance than the presidential race. Anyone with a theory about the importance of running for seats in the U.S. Senate, state legislatures, or community power boards will also find no opposition here. You might even say that this book is premised on the idea that, so far as political activity goes, there is no such thing as a "theory of everything."

It is a simple fact of life that all of the levels of government have serious impacts on people's lives. School class size, state tax policy, drone warfare – all of these issues deal with things that are happening now, all at the same time. We have to deal with it all now, at the same time. So just as this book makes no case that presidential primary politics take precedence over any number of other important political activities, the only argument it rejects in this realm is the idea that the importance of one of the other levels of government is paramount, to the point that it demands our staying out of national politics, whether permanently or even just temporarily until some future point when we think we've somehow gotten some other level of electoral politics in hand.

If we are at all serious about changing America's course in the world – now – we have to take the debate to the top – now. There's no one else who's going to do it for us if we don't. The national political figures whom we continually deride for not discussing what needs to be discussed are not going to miraculously start doing so unless we force them to. But if we consider it bad news that we don't have the luxury of being able to just think about one thing at a time or to "work our way up" from the bottom, the good news is that any waves we make on the national level will probably only make it easier to rock the boat at the local level – and vice versa.

The Primary Route

Move Them to the Left by Making Them Lose If They Don't

This argument doesn't often make it into print, but it's out there nonetheless: the idea that we should go with third party politics and run presidential candidates who'll take our point of view into the final election campaign. If these campaigns prove successful enough, the Democrats may perceive a shift of their vote away from them and toward that third party. If that shift should prove big enough to hurt, presumably by facilitating a Republican presidential win, or at least raising the prospect of facilitating one, the Democrats will have no choice but to follow the electorate and move in the direction of the party that lured their voters away, presumably to the left in this discussion.

Perhaps the closest this idea comes to actually making an appearance in American political history as an operative theory is in a rumor concerning Huey Long. Some of his biographers suggest that Long, then a Democratic Senator from Louisiana who had announced his intention to run for president, recognized that he would not be able to pry the Democratic nomination away from FDR in 1936, but hoped to see another candidate run a third party campaign much like the one that William Lemke actually did run as the Union Party candidate, but much more successful, to the point where it would siphon off enough votes from Roosevelt to tip the election to the Republicans.[40] The plan was that in 1940 Long would then win the Democratic nomination and ultimately the presidency itself. Long was assassinated before any of this could happen, though, so this rumor is at most an historical foot note.

We have, however, more recently witnessed a situation that provided a reasonable facsimile of how a strategy like that might have played out, even though it was not the intent in this particular race. The question of whether Ralph Nader bore responsibility for George Bush's election in 2000 has been hotly debated ever since. Even today it's still easy to find people who claim that the Nader candidacy actually did "cost" Al Gore the presidency and it's just as easy to find people who think that claim has no merit. What you will not easily find, however, is anyone who maintains that the 2000 election caused the Democratic Party to read the handwriting on the wall and conclude that it needed to shift to the left in pursuit of Nader's base – in 2004 or any subsequent year. Equally hard to locate is anyone who believes that the Nader campaign succeeded in developing any kind of new alternative to the Democratic Party on the left.

Vote Em In; Vote Em Out

Then there's what I'll call the "vote em in, vote em out" stance, the idea being that people concerned with changing the country in a serious way are best off not devoting too much time to the electoral process at all, because it will likely just sap our energy, if not compromise us hopelessly. Better we should devote our time to non-electoral organizing on the issues that matter. If we are successful, the politicians will follow; those are the ones we vote for. If they won't follow, we vote against them. While this may not qualify as a political theory, variants of this point of view do appear to be firmly held and widespread among Americans, even those with an abiding interest in social change.

If nothing else, this apolitical approach to politics does at least have the virtue of being a pretty effective description of much of the actual history of the American left. But if you've gotten this far in this book, chances are that you think that this history could have been significantly improved upon. This particular wrinkle of American exceptionalist political theory does seem a logical enough reaction to the exceptionally American political reality of having two parties governing the country within an extremely circumscribed range of political debate. But ultimately it only re-poses the question that led us here: Do we continue on as virtually the only country that has a reasonably open democratic system yet has no substantial political organization or tendency that consistently brings a pro-economic democracy/anti-militarist viewpoint directly to the voters in national elections?

Electoral politics may not be for everyone and presidential politics may not even be for everyone who is involved in electoral politics, but if some of us don't take on the task of bringing the ideas of the left before a national audience, who will? Want American political debate to remain exceptionally narrow? Just keep on voting them in and voting them out – and leave it at that.

The Value of Third Parties

Envisioning a way forward for the American left demands that we pay close attention to the specifics of our system. But just as we cannot take third party success stories from elsewhere in the world and superimpose them on our very different system, we shouldn't fail to see that there are places among the nation's disparate political structures where third parties can achieve success and have already done so.

In his 2002 book on America's third parties, *Spoiling For a Fight*, journalist Micah Sifry judged that among the various third parties there were only three "with serious aspirations of reaching the broader citizenry"[41] on the national level – the Greens, Libertarians and the New Party – to which he added "three of the existing single-state parties – Minnesota's Independence Party, Vermont's Progressive Party, and New York's Working Families Party."[42]

The Greens

The 2000 Nader campaign obviously did not work out as a growth opportunity for the Green Party on the national level. The Greens have nonetheless experienced some success in a number of localities.

In the rich tapestry of local election systems in use across this country, there are many that are not dominated by the "subtractive" element that has been so difficult for third parties to overcome in the higher level elections. It is not uncommon for local elections to involve some type of non-partisan, two-round process that treats a third party candidate exactly the same as a Democrat or a Republican. So if your candidate does not make it

The Value of Third Parties

to the runoff round, you vote for your favorite of the ones that did – or the "lesser of the two evils" – regardless of the parties involved. Most successful third party candidacies have come in races of this type.

In 2015, the Green Party listed 122 of its members as officeholders in 23 states.[43] They included members of the Berkeley, California Rent Stabilization Board; Fairfield, Connecticut Zoning Board of Appeals (Alternate); Hillsborough County, Florida Soil & Water Conservation District (Alternate); Amherst, Massachusetts Town Meeting; Minneapolis, Minnesota City Council; Lower Platte, Nebraska Natural Resources District; and the Rutherford, New Jersey School Board. Greens also served as Mayor of New Paltz, New York; Brookfield, Massachusetts Selectman; Loudon, Virginia Soil & Water Conservation District Director; Mississippi County, Arkansas Justice of the Peace; and Constable of Redding, Connecticut.

At one time or another, Greens have constituted the majority on three city councils in California and one in New York, and have also formed the majority of a California school board. They have also elected a mayor in Richmond, California, a city with a population over 100,000, for two consecutive terms and she was only prevented from seeking a third by term limits.

Historically, local governments have been the venues of all manner of cross-party cooperation of a sort rarely found on the national level. An interesting example occurred in 2003 in San Francisco at the time the city had a non-partisan two-round mayoral election. A Green candidate, Board of Supervisors President Matt Gonzalez, made it into the runoff against Gavin Newsom, the establishment Democrat candidate who was also a member of the Board. At that point, two of the city's anti-establishment Democratic clubs opted to endorse the Green. Although Newsom won, some mainstream Democrats were incensed by this break in party ranks. Individual Central Committee members who had endorsed Gonzalez found themselves the object of a coordinated campaign run against them when they sought reelection to that body and a move was also made to de-charter the two maverick clubs. Ultimately, this

163

attempt failed, probably because one of the clubs, the Harvey Milk Lesbian-Gay-Bisexual-Transgender Democratic Club, was the city's largest and most important and its expulsion would have damaged the city's Democratic Party as a whole.[44] An unintended and ironic result of the failed effort to expel the wayward clubs was that it established the right of Democratic Clubs to endorse non-Democrats in future non-partisan primaries.[45]

Third Parties on the State Level

Some states use a two-round system for state government elections and even for Congress. Although this structure is generally more favorable to third party candidacies that the more commonly used single round elections, these states, mostly in the south, have thus far produced few notable third party successes. There have been some significant third party or independent successes elsewhere, though, such as former pro wrestler Jesse Ventura's 1998 election as governor of Minnesota. Sustaining those third parties has generally been a greater challenge and in 2014, the Minnesota Independence Party, on whose line Ventura was elected and about which Micah Sifry wrote, lost its permanent place on the ballot when its gubernatorial candidate received just 2.88 percent of the vote.

The Vermont Progressive Party is currently the most successful stand-alone (as opposed to fusion) third party in the country. Its origins are in Bernie Sanders's campaigns for mayor of Burlington, Vermont, although he never formally affiliated with the party. After the 2014 election the Vermont Progressives held one of 30 state senate seats and six of 150 house seats. The party's 2014 lieutenant gubernatorial candidate drew 36 percent of the vote, winning the endorsement of the major Democratic office holders when the Democrats did not field a candidate of their own. Additionally, five of fourteen seats on the Burlington City Council are held by Progressives, along with three other local offices.

Third Parties on the National Level

The most noteworthy recent exception to the general rule

The Value of Third Parties

of third party failure on the federal level has been Bernie Sanders' election to the House of Representatives, then later to the Senate from the state of Vermont. Sanders's achievement must rank as extraordinary, so the particulars are worth noting. With about 625,000 inhabitants, Vermont is the second least populous of the fifty states, one of seven represented by only a single member in the House of Representatives.

After running five state-wide races during which his vote increased from 2.2% to 14.4%, Sanders – who had in the interim been elected mayor of Burlington, the state's largest city – ran for the U.S. House in 1988. He drew 37.5% of the vote; the Republican won and the Democrat finished third. Two years later, he defeated the incumbent Republican with 56% of the vote, as the Democrat received only 3%. Subsequently, Democrats have generally not challenged him, and when they have, none has received more than 9.3% of the vote. Over time then, Sanders – the longest serving independent member of Congress in U.S. history – has overcome the "subtractive" aspect of the plurality election system and essentially replaced the Democratic Party in the races in which he has run.[46]

While we clearly shouldn't deny the modest but real successes that third parties have achieved in local and even state elections, we cannot afford to ignore the specific circumstances of those victories and assume that they can be replicated in the national election process. Unquestionably there have been and will continue to be situations where third parties offer clear and tangible advantages over working within the Democratic Party, situations in which it is much easier to achieve political clarity and coherence working as a separate party than it would be operating as a caucus, formal or informal, within the Democratic Party. One of the few downsides of these local third party victories actually may be that people come to believe that the presidential election process could work the same way, only on a larger scale.

And as for the great exception to the rule, the independent career of Bernie Sanders, we should note that he has actually caucused with the Democrats in Congress and, more significantly,

The Primary Route

that so far as presidential politics go, he has never promoted the third party or independent route, declining even to endorse Ralph Nader in 2000. And, of course, he has now decided to take precisely the route this book argues and enter the Democratic presidential primaries.

One thing we can be sure of about the future is that it won't play out according to anyone's plan. It is conceivable that hybrid political groups could someday develop that might choose to operate as third parties running independent candidates on the local and/or state level while simultaneously supporting Democrats in the presidential primaries. While an arrangement like this risks creating additional confusion for the voter, we'd probably we wise never to say, "never."

Other Electoral Reforms

There are currently reformers actively promoting any number of changes to our political system that are designed to democratize, simplify or clarify the electoral process. Among the most significant are instant runoff voting, abolition of the electoral college, and fusion.

Instant Runoff Voting

Instant runoff or ranked choice voting, which allows voters to rank more than choices for an office, largely eliminates the need for tactical voting, i.e. voting for someone other than your actual preferred candidate based upon an assessment that your first choice has little chance of winning. Any number of variants of this system have been formulated and several have been enacted. These systems are mostly to be found on the municipal level, but several southern states have recently offered that option, for federal races, to absentee voters living abroad.

Abolishing the Electoral College

Like the U.S. Senate, which was not directly elected at the outset, the Electoral College was part of the "Founding Fathers'" design for a government structure that would be democratic, but not *too* democratic. And while our Senators are no longer selected by the various state legislatures, the byzantine structure of the Electoral College has survived all efforts to replace it. [47] Consequently, the American presidency has gone to the runner-up rather than to the candidate who actually received the highest number of votes on four separate occasions – in 1824, 1876, 1888 and 2000. (Since the founding of the Republican Party, all three of those second-place wins have gone to them, by the way.) Over the years, numerous constitutional amendments have been introduced to replace the Electoral College with a direct popular vote determining the presidency, but none has passed both branches of Congress.

The most interesting current reform effort sidesteps Congress entirely. The National Popular Vote bill, introduced in numerous states, commits the states that enact it to direct their electors to vote for the winner of the overall national popular vote, regardless of which candidate has won a plurality in their particular states. The law would only take effect when it has been enacted by a group of states with a cumulative vote total sufficient to control the Electoral College, which is to say at least 270 electoral votes.

As of this writing it has been enacted by 10 states and the District of Columbia, a group that commands 165 electoral votes — 61% of the total needed to activate the laws in the various states that have passed it.

Fusion

The most significant "additive" innovation developed over the course of America's presidential election history has been fusion, the name given to various methods of combining the votes and support of two or more political parties behind a single candidate.

The fusion process was fairly common in nineteenth century politics. Its most noteworthy appearance in the presidential arena came in 1892 when the People's Party, the Populists, unified with the Democrats in several western and midwestern states. Its effects were substantial, as People's Party candidate James Weaver became, along with Robert La Follette, one of only two third party candidates whom we might consider "left wing" to carry entire states and therefore actually win electoral votes.

Other Electoral Reforms

Reaction to this development was swift, however, as state legislatures began to ban fusion. As a Republican legislator from Minnesota put it, "We don't propose to allow the Democrats to make allies of the Populists, Prohibitionists, or any other party, and get up combination tickets against us. We can whip them single-handed, but don't intend to fight all creation."[48]

Eventually 18 states banned fusion. And as was so often the case, fusion politics sometimes took a different course in the South, where there were actually instances of Populist-Republican fusion. In 1896, for instance, although its voters generally supported William Jennings Bryan in the presidential election, the North Carolina People's Party actually fused with the Republicans on state level politics.

For much of the twentieth century, one of the few states where fusion politics flourished was New York, most notably with the American Labor Party (ALP) and, later, the Liberal Party. The ALP originated with a group of dissident Socialist Party members who were concerned by the possibility that Socialist Party presidential candidate Norman Thomas, who had received 200,000 votes in New York state in the 1932 election, might emerge as a spoiler to Roosevelt in 1936. The ALP was conceived as an opportunity to vote for Franklin Roosevelt *and* for a party to the left of the Democrats – a way of expressing a kind of dissenting support. Over the next two decades, the party backed successful Democratic *and* Republican candidates and sent Vito Marcantonio to Congress. In 1948 the ALP declined to back the reelection of Democratic President Harry Truman, instead supporting Progressive Henry Wallace and providing a substantial portion of his total national vote. The party backed the Progressive presidential candidate in 1952 as well and dissolved after losing its place on the ballot for failing to secure the requisite number of votes in 1954.

The ALP was supplanted by the Liberal Party, founded in 1944 by ALP members who objected to Communist influence in their old party. Although the Liberals started with national ambitions, the party wound up functioning almost exclusively in

The Primary Route

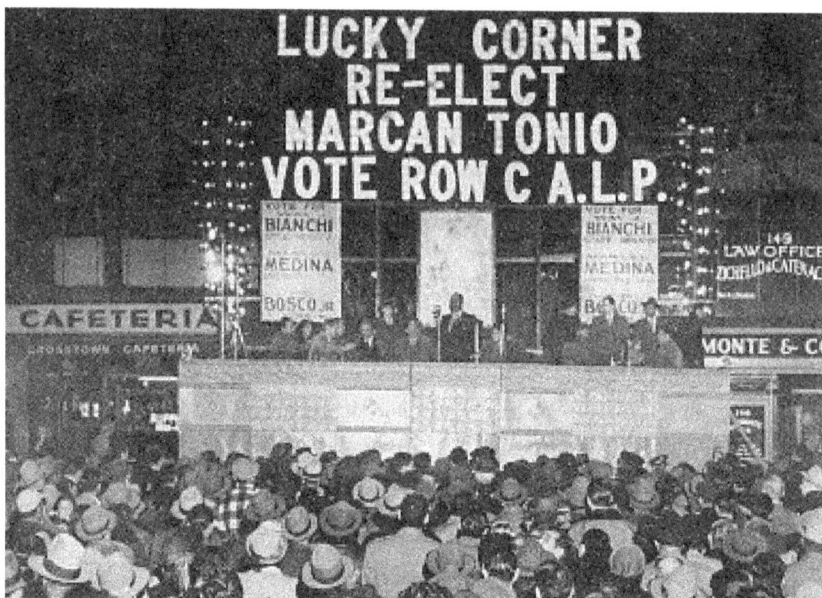

Congressman Vito Marcantonio opposed the Korean War and promoted civil rights as a member of the American Labor Party.

New York and enjoying considerable successes – John Lindsay was reelected mayor of New York City in 1969 based primarily on Liberal Party votes after failing to be renominated in the Republican primary – before it too lost its place on the ballot in 2002.

A significant effort to revive the fusion process on a national level was mounted in the 1990s with the creation of the New Party. The initial proposal was to create "a cross between the 'party within the party' strategy favored by some Democratic Party activists and the 'plague on both your houses' stance adopted by some who were critics of both major parties."[49] When the state of Minnesota ruled against the New Party's right to endorse a Democratic Farmer-Labor candidate, the party went to court claiming that fusion was a constitutionally protected exercise of the right to free association. The case went all the way to the U.S. Supreme Court which ruled against that argument in the 1997 case *Timmons v. Twin Cities Area New Party.* In his majority opinion, Chief Justice William Rehnquist wrote that, "The Constitution

Other Electoral Reforms

permits the Minnesota Legislature to decide that political stability is best served through a healthy two-party system" – without noting just where the Constitution referred to the "two-party system."

Although nothing prevents the various states from amending their election law to permit fusion (seven other states allow it, in addition to New York), the court decision effectively ended the New Party effort. As usual in this regard, however, New York remains the exception where fusion continues to be a living process. Under New York state law candidates with multiple endorsements are listed on multiple party lines on the ballot and the vote from each of them is then subsequently tallied. The relative contribution of each party endorsement is therefore obvious. Under some other states' election laws, the candidate with multiple party is listed but once, along with the names of the endorsing parties. This method, sometimes known as "aggregated fusion," provides no opportunity to sort out the contributions of the several parties, no chance for a party to count its support, demonstrate its importance, or measure its growth.

In New York, the left-wing Working Families Party (WFP) has largely come to fill the niche once occupied by the American Labor and Liberal Parties. Governor-elect Andrew Cuomo received over 150,000 votes on the party's line in 2010. That campaign did, however, also highlight the frailties inherent in a fusion party's existence, when the Democrat Cuomo initially rejected the WFP endorsement as part of a process of forcing the smaller party to alter its program so as not to conflict with his policy preferences. Since a party needs to receive at least 50,000 votes to maintain its place on the State of New York's ballot, Cuomo correctly assessed the situation as one where the WFP needed him more than he needed the WFP, and he was largely successful in his efforts to bend the party to his will.

The WFP will occasionally endorse liberal Republicans and in unusual circumstances may even run a candidate of its own. In 2003 a WFP candidate became the first person in thirty years to be elected to the New York City Council from a third party. In 2015, a WFP candidate from Brooklyn won a four-way State

The Primary Route

Assembly race in the absence of a Democratic Party candidate in the race. The WFP is also very active in Connecticut, which has a weaker form of fusion.

Fusion efforts have also persisted in other states. In 2006, the Mass Ballot Freedom Campaign placed a Fusion Voting Initiative on the ballot in Massachusetts. It received 30.7% of the vote. In 2009, Oregon passed legislation allowing for "aggregated fusion" and the Independent Party of Oregon has since used the law to support candidates.

Campaign Finance Reform

Numerous thoughtful books have been written on the topic of reforming our system of financing political campaigns in the U.S.A. There is no need, then, for this book to revisit what has been and is being done well elsewhere. Suffice it to say, however, that any measures that move toward the public financing of campaigns and limiting the power of big money in American elections are entirely in tune with the overall thrust of this book. It is almost impossible to imagine that any presidential candidacy that had at its core the question of reducing our national disparities of income, wealth and power would not be raising the questions of campaign funding fairness, on a daily basis.

Conclusion

As was the case with the question of whether electoral activity on one level of government took priority over activity on any other, so far as reform of the electoral process goes, this book advocates a multi-track approach. To recognize that the American left can never achieve maximum political impact without becoming a significant factor in the presidential election debate does not in any way imply that we need to postpone the pursuit of important electoral reforms to some indefinite future time when we have mastered the primary process. The adoption of strong New York-style fusion laws, the abolition of the Electoral College, the reshaping of our voting processes in a direction that enhances the system's *additive* aspects and de-emphasizes its *subtractive* side,

Other Electoral Reforms

and above all, meaningful campaign finance reforms are all changes that we need *yesterday*. At the same time, we cannot assume that they will happen *tomorrow*. And we must make the fight to change America *today*

.

2016 and the Shape of Things to Come

For a point of reference, let us revisit the year 2004, the last time that a candidate of the left, Dennis Kucinich, made a start-to-finish race in the presidential primary process. That year Kucinich was outshone in the public eye by a center-left candidate, Howard Dean. As an activist who came down on the Kucinich side of that particular divide, this writer also recognizes that the dividing lines between political campaigns are written in sand, porous, malleable and often rubbed out when a particular candidate enters or leaves the fray. It's one thing for us to agree on principle that "we" should have "our" candidate in the thick of the presidential debate; it may be quite another thing to agree on should actually be the one who's in the thick of it.

For a lot of people, the question of which candidate to support in an election, even a presidential election, may come down to a snap judgement. People who generally see eye to eye on most things suddenly find themselves in different camps. As the old saw has it, in politics there are "no permanent friends, no permanent enemies" – tomorrow you may well need the support of the person with whom you find yourself at odds today. The reason *why* people committed to a candidate can be more significant than *which* particular campaign it actually was.

Keeping that 2004 election in mind, the target audience of this book has three parts. It obviously includes those who supported Kucinich in that race – as well as those who would have supported his campaign but either were not aware of him or were not yet of political age at the time. It also includes those who opted for Dean, or would have, because they thought that backing the more viable candidate might better advance the antiwar cause.

2016 and the Shape of Things To Come

The third group is those who didn't – or wouldn't – even ask the "Kucinich or Dean?" question because they were, or are, third party advocates who couldn't, or can't, see their way clear to supporting any Democrat.

Beyond?

Eventually, we could imagine, or at least hope, that if presidential candidacies of the left were ever to become a routine and expected thing, the ad hoc, self-selecting aspect of the current nominating process might come to be seen as insufficiently democratic. We might envision a desire for something of a more participatory candidate selection process down the road, perhaps some form of organization that could maintain a measure of continuity from one presidential election cycle to the next.

Among the questions we can only hope we'll be fortunate enough to have to face in future years are:

Is there a way to carry the achievements of one campaign forward four years later, or is the American left doomed to a permanent time loop of starting from scratch every four years like the Bill Murray character in the movie *Groundhog Day*?

Will candidates continue to devise their own personal issues list each time out or could we hope to see them running within a broad pre-existing framework of "left" issues that transcend individual campaigns and become an regular part of the presidential process?

Will presidential campaigns always remain an essentially individual entrepreneurial venture or are there organizations that would be willing to sign onto a process that continued from candidate to candidate, campaign to campaign?

Is there a possibility of developing a "party within the party" on an ongoing basis?

Is it possible and worthwhile to reinvigorate the convention and platform processes?

Can an ongoing left tendency in presidential politics walk the fine line of being challenging, but not self-defeating? Willing to compromise while not abandoning basic principles?

The Primary Route

These are real problems, posing questions without pre-existing answers. They are precisely the sort of the problems we want to have, however. They are the problems of a successful movement.

Given that we're now in the third century of our country's existence, more than a hundred years since the introduction of the primary system, and we've yet to master the presidential election process, there seems little reason to think that the American left will suddenly, smoothly, and in a hurry find its way to making a permanent place for itself in the main event. Mounting even a single left presidential primary campaign is an immense task in itself, but here at least we have some precedents to learn from. As for attempting to maintain some continuity from one left presidential candidate to the next, however, there is no precedent.

The three candidates whose campaigns constitute the core background to this book – Jesse Jackson, Ralph Nader and Dennis Kucinich – each ran more than one presidential campaign. So we do at least have some experience of continuity in the consecutive campaigns run by the same candidate (although, unfortunately, Jackson's 1988 campaign offers the only obvious example of one of them successfully building upon a prior effort). But that's it – beyond the persistence of an individual candidate running a second time, there's nothing. Thus far, each of our presidential campaigns has been essentially a made-to-order entrepreneurial venture, built from scratch and organized for one-time use to advance a specific candidate.

The presidential candidates of today do visit and consult with the individual and organizational "players" of campaigns past, so there is a certain amount of carry over maintained in that process, but ongoing public coalitions designed to carry a presidential political agenda on from one four-year period to the next are pretty much unknown in our history. And the particular nature of our presidential election system leaves us with no really obvious parallel in any other country to turn to for ideas.

176

2016 and the Shape of Things To Come

A party within the party?

The idea of creating a sort of "party within the party" has surfaced periodically on the American left among those who are disaffected with actually existing two-party politics but do not see third party politics as a viable option. The gist of the concept has generally been to recognize and identify some common purpose among pro-economic democracy/anti-militarist activists who have an interest in government. Any organization that might develop from this might not have any specific formal affiliation with the Democratic Party, but as a practical matter most of the individuals involved *would* have some sort of affiliation with it, if only in the fact that they were very unlikely to be Republicans. The more ambitious visions have imagined harmonizing the agendas of disparate but compatible organizations and causes into a coherent political tendency capable of exerting an appeal broader than the sum of its parts. For the most part, though, "party within the party" discussions have focused on the legislative branch of government – Congress or the various state legislatures, with presidential elections rarely making it onto the agenda.

With so little historical precedent for, or even consideration of, the idea of an organization centered around presidential politics that is not actually a separate political party, it's far from certain that an entity like that could ever even take root in American politics. Still, it's probably worthwhile to consider what's out there now that might suggest how we could hope to do it over the long run, even if it may be too early to start thinking about installing the phones.

The Coalition

A successful, long-running presidential campaign coalition would likely have to balance the interests and support of at least three types of institutions: unions, which bring the solidest base and financing; elected officials, who have practical governmental and electoral experience; and a broad array of membership and issues organizations.

The Primary Route

Unions

American unions have been in steady decline as a percentage of the population they represent since their peak in 1954, when 34.8% of all U.S. wage and salary workers belonged to one. By 1983, their ranks had fallen to 20.1% of the workforce and by 2013 the figure was only 11.3%. But even that reduced 2013 percentage translated into 14.5 million members, a big decline from their highest total membership of 21.0 million in 1979, but still making unions the country's most important working class institutions by far. And their reach was actually broader than the membership, in that about another 1.5 million non-union members worked under union contracts.

The percentage of union membership varies widely from location to location and industry to industry, ranging, in 2013 from a low of 3.0 percent in North Carolina to a high of 24.4 percent in New York. Men are more likely to belong than women, although the gap has narrowed significantly: In 1983, 24.7 percent of male workers were in unions, compared to 14.6 percent of women; in 2013, the respective rates were 11.9 percent and 10.5 percent.

Older workers are more commonly in unions: 14.0% of workers ages 45 to 54 belong and 14.3 percent of those 55 to 64. By race, blacks have the highest rate of union membership – 13.6 percent in 2013, followed by whites at 11.0 percent, and Asians and Hispanics, both at 9.4 percent.

At their highpoint, American unions primarily represented private sector workers, with public employee participation less than 10%. Over time, the relative membership rates have reversed. Now about 36% of public workers belong to unions, with the highest concentration, 40.8 percent, in local government. Overall private sector membership has fallen below 7%, with the highest concentration in utilities, 25.6%; transportation and warehousing, 19.6%; telecommunications, 14.4%; and construction, 14.1%. Unionization is virtually non-existent (about one percent) in finance, food service and agriculture, the celebrated campaigns of Cesar Chavez and the United Farmworkers notwithstanding.

The decline in the percentage of workers with union representation has transformed the nature of union activities.

2016 and the Shape of Things To Come

Strikes have virtually disappeared: In 1970 there were 381 major strikes and lockouts; in 1980 there were 187; in 2010 only 11, a decline of 97% over forty years. At the same time unions have increased their activity in politics. Union members tend to vote at a higher rate than the general population and the AFL-CIO has estimated that in some elections about one in four voters comes from a union household. It also estimates that 68% to 74% of its members vote along with leadership recommendations.

According to the Center for Responsive Politics, in the 1992 election cycle unions made $52,949,275 in federal campaign contributions, 94% of it to Democrats. In 2008, the figure was $75,826,442, with 92% going to Democrats. In 2012, the total went way up to $141,319,719, with 90% to Democrats.[50] In the 2012 election cycle, labor also spent an additional $46,390,734 on lobbying on the federal level.[51] When it comes to presidential politics, labor unions participate in a big way. The challenge in this sector is to convince the labor movement that backing the candidates they *really* would prefer, even if they're not going to win immediately, can actually be part of a realistic and ultimately fruitful long run strategy.

To keep everything in perspective, labor may loom large on the left, but in the larger political arena it is thoroughly dwarfed by business interests. The Center for Responsive Politics estimates that in the 2013-2014 federal election cycle, business outspent labor by $1,571,432,082 to $132,469,709 and notes that, "The broadest classification of political donors separates them into business, labor, or ideological interests. Whatever slice you look at, business interests dominate, with an overall advantage over organized labor of about 15-to-1.

"Even among PACs - the favored means of delivering funds by labor unions - business has a more than 3-to-1 fundraising advantage. In soft money, the ratio is nearly 17-to-1."[52]

By all indications, this disparity is only likely to increase. The Freedom Partners Chamber of Commerce, the political organization of the Koch brothers, who control Koch Industries, the second largest privately-owned company in the United States, has announced its intention to spend $889 million on the 2016 elections.[53]

The Progressive Caucus

The Congressional Progressive Caucus is the most likely prototype of an American electoral left of the future. Arguably one of the most important political organizations in the country, although relatively little known among the public at large, it was founded in 1991 by six U.S. House members: Tom Andrews (D-ME), Peter DeFazio (D-OR), Ron Dellums (D-CA), Lane Evans (D-IL), Bernie Sanders (I-VT) and Maxine Waters (D-CA). The Caucus now has seventy-five House members, making it the largest caucus in the House, and one Senator (Sanders).

The Caucus operates on a four-point statement of principles called the Progressive Promise that hews fairly closely to the general list of concerns at the beginning of this book:

1. Fighting for economic justice and security for all;

2. Protecting and preserving our civil rights and civil liberties;

3. Promoting global peace and security; and

4. Advancing environmental protection and energy independence.

The Caucus produces an annual alternate budget proposal. Its most recent one, the Back to Work Budget, called for immediately allowing the Bush tax cuts to expire for families earning over $250K, raising the tax rates for millionaires and billionaires from 45% to 49%, taxing income from investments at the same rate as income from wages, enacting a financial transactions tax, and returning Pentagon spending to the 2006 level. It also maintains an organization, Progressive Congress, whose stated goal is "building lasting infrastructure that bridges the gap between progressives in Congress and the rest of the progressive infrastructure nationwide."

The "Issues" Organizations

While America's unions constitute the most important

180

counterweight to the country's dominant corporations, their cumulative weight is nonetheless far from sufficient to carry the day politically. Fortunately there are also a dizzying array of "issues organizations" working largely outside of the electoral arena that are trying to reach the remainder of the "99%" on the concerns central to this book. This sector is mentioned last simply because it is the hardest to define and to organize, and not because it counts least in importance. In fact, in terms of both their current importance and their future potential, it is these disparate groups, and others they may spawn, that will probably hold the key to any future transformation of American politics from the presidential level on down.

The Progressive Congress maintains a list of what it calls its "additional key partners" that may give some idea of the breadth of interests that will need to be incorporated into any effort to wrest American politics from corporate dominance.[54] And this list represents just the tip of the proverbial iceberg. For instance, *Wikipedia* lists 140 separate environmental and conservation organizations in the United States, along with 67 civil rights organizations. And those are just the national organizations. How many currently exist on the state and local levels is anyone's guess. To take the single state of Massachusetts, the Campaign for Single Payer Health Care (MASS-CARE) counts 86 separate organizations as part of its coalition.

As indicated at the outset, this book makes no predictions. Will the American left actually start to take presidential elections, and specifically presidential primaries, more seriously than it has in the past, as this book advocates? Can it pull together a significant, but declining, labor movement; independent political operatives; and unconnected issues organizations into a force capable of steering a new course for the nation? We don't know – and certainly we can't assume that it will happen because this book says it should. Will the American left meet with success if it does attempt to systematically engage with the presidential election process? Again, we can't know. But while it may never be possible to be sure of success, failure can be guaranteed.

The Primary Route

In that vein, this book does make one prediction: If the American left does not find its voice within the presidential election process it will remain but a marginal force in American life. We may score excellent debating points from the sidelines, but we will not actually be a part of the debate.

A Personal Introduction

(at the end of the book)

There is a fundamental irony at the core of this book. It is obviously written by a highly political person for a highly political audience, and yet it avoids taking anything but the most general political stances. It maintains the primacy of issues in politics and yet it largely confines itself to making an argument about the mechanics of our political system. So there's nothing about, for instance, my particular position on the Israel/Palestine question because I don't want potential disagreement on specific issues, no matter how important those specifics might be, to obscure broader areas of agreement. If you think that the U.S. spends too little money on its own citizens and too much on foreign wars, then my argument is aimed at prodding you toward a certain course of action designed to make that general perspective a more important part of American politics – regardless of how many specific questions we may disagree on.

A similar consideration lies behind my decision to place a personal introduction at the end rather than the beginning of the book. Since this book grew out of a life-long interest in presidential politics in which an intuition about the importance of the presidential primaries grew into a conviction that those primaries were central to the prospects of any potential American electoral left, I thought it might be to the point to describe the path that led me to this conclusion. But I feared that telling that story up front ran the risk of providing too many potential points of disagreement. I didn't want to give cause for someone to think, *"This guy supported (fill in the blank) in that election? That's ridiculous, I'm not reading any more."* But now that I've made my argument in the abstract, I am going to give you a bit of the specifics, not with the idea of convincing the reader that all of my

The Primary Route

answers were right, but to convey a sense of the questions that I, and many other like-minded people, asked in election seasons of the past.

My interest in presidential campaigns goes back for about as long as I've had interests in anything. I turned eight during the first presidential campaign that I remember. It was 1956 and, as the campaign buttons said, *I liked Ike*, a.k.a. Dwight D. Eisenhower. Yes, my first candidate was a Republican. I assume the reason for this was that my parents liked Adlai Stevenson, so I wanted to be for the other guy. I was, after all, already a lifelong-to-be Brooklyn Dodger fan living in the Bronx. My fling with the Grand Old Party didn't last long, however. In 1960, the force of the nomination of the Irish Catholic John Kennedy proved of sufficient weight to overcome even my resistance to agreeing with my parents and brought me into the Democratic fold, along with everyone else who had been waiting for this second coming since Al Smith's nomination in 1928. I was never to support a Republican presidential candidate again.

By 1964, the presidential election thing was actually getting serious for me. Now a junior in a Catholic high school in Manhattan so conservative that Barry Goldwater won the school-wide presidential straw poll, I was eagerly out of sync with my classmates, to the tune of attending not one but two Lyndon Johnson rallies in Madison Square Garden, one for the Democrats and one for the Liberals, New York being a "fusion" state.

My trajectory to the left did not stop there though and by 1968, now a junior in college, the Vietnam War had moved me from my "All the Way with LBJ" stance of 1964 to demonstrations where people chanted, "Hey, hey, LBJ! How many kids did you kill today?" Those of us under 21 didn't yet have the vote. If we had, I would have voted for Minnesota Senator Eugene McCarthy in the primary, because, unlike New York Senator Robert Kennedy, McCarthy had been the one willing to take on LBJ on the Vietnam War and demonstrate the president's vulnerability – which then drew Kennedy into the race. And by the time it came down to the Nixon-Humphrey, pick-your-Vietnam War-supporter final election, I was pretty firmly in the "Vote with your feet; vote in the street" camp. But, again, I was only 20, so it was all just theoretical.

The first presidential vote I did get to cast was for South Dakota Senator George McGovern in 1972, and I don't think I've ever cast a better one. I didn't work for his campaign, at least not directly, since I was still pretty well alienated from the national Democratic Party at that point. Fortunately Tom Hayden and Jane Fonda had come up with a program for people who fit that description – the Indochina Peace Campaign, an organization that operated entirely independently of the Democrats in a number of states that would be electorally important for McGovern, a sort of parallel McGovern campaign for leftists. I spent the campaign working for that organization, mostly shipping boxes of campaign literature out of the New York office to those electorally significant states. As you may know, our efforts did not turn that election. Election night was crushing. They called Nixon the winner before I even had time to drink myself silly. My only consolation was that I got the nastiest drunk of my life out of the way at a relatively young age.

The next couple of presidential campaigns went by in a kind of a whoosh for me. In 1976, former Oklahoma Senator Fred Harris caught my eye. But although he had been working at it for awhile, by the time the race actually started I think he was out of it before I could even get around to figuring out how to get involved in his campaign. In 1980, I was running my own second, and first winning, campaign for Massachusetts State Representative, so I was pretty well tied up in that. But still, it seems some kind of measure of how relatively unmoved I was by Senator Ted Kennedy's challenge to President Jimmy Carter that year, that I don't actually remember voting for him, although I suppose I must have.

In 1984, however, I wound up with a surprise second chance at working for McGovern for president. And this time I took it – in a campaign that virtually no one remembers today. McGovern was not actually my first candidate in that election, which is not to say that he wasn't my first choice. Thinking this could well be the only presidential campaign during which I'd be holding political office, a correct assessment, as it turned out, I had

The Primary Route

decided I'd try to do the whole presidential election thing to the hilt and get in early. Early meant 1983, when the field consisted of former Vice President Walter Mondale, Colorado Senator Gary Hart and California Senator Alan Cranston. Of the three, Cranston was considered the peace candidate, so I signed on with him and actually was named co-chair of his Massachusetts campaign and even did a campaign trip to New Hampshire, where my time was generally wasted.

A funny thing happened while all of this was going on, though – George McGovern entered the race, although he wasn't being taken terribly seriously. I actually much preferred McGovern's platform to Cranston's, but I was committed – statewide co-chair, for chrissake! – so I just had to keep the blinders on and try not to think too much about McGovern.[55]

And then came the Iowa caucuses. The Cranston staffers I knew who had been to Iowa had told me that Cranston, who represented the agribusiness state of California, just hadn't understood that farm parity was very much a live issue in the midwest. Like me, he apparently thought it was something out of your nineteenth century history lessons. But the South Dakotan George McGovern knew that it wasn't. And he then actually beat Cranston in Iowa, even though it was Cranston who was supposed to be the "serious" candidate.

After another disappointing showing in the New Hampshire primary, Cranston dropped out, which set up one of my favorite memories of my legislative years, and one of my favorite political memories of any year. When I arrived at my State House office on the day after the New Hampshire Primary, I found two messages on my desk – one from the Mondale campaign, the other from the Hart campaign, both of them presumably trying to scoop up bodies tumbling off the Cranston bandwagon. Dramatically crumpling both notes in my left hand, I dialed Information with my right, got the McGovern headquarters number, called them up, and offered my support.

McGovern had not done terribly well in New Hampshire himself, so he had announced that he would make his stand in Massachusetts, the only state he'd carried against Richard Nixon

A Personal Introduction

in 1972. He was going to forego campaigning in the other eight states that were also holding Super Tuesday primaries and if he did not win, or at least run a close second in Massachusetts, he would drop out of the race. My belated endorsement was his first from a Massachusetts legislator, and his last. In fact, a member of a local electric power board and I would represent the extent of his support among elected officials in the state. Which meant that I was asked to introduce him at several campaign rallies, including one particularly memorable one in Boston's Faneuil Hall.

At the time, I considered those last two weeks of George McGovern's final political campaign a peak political experience and my appreciation of it has only been enhanced by the fact that in the intervening years my estimation of his 1972 campaign has only grown, as it has outshone every campaign that followed. You don't often get second shots in life, but in this case I did.[56]

Unfortunately, however, McGovern was good to his word and dropped out of the presidential race after finishing a strong *third* in Massachusetts. By the day after Super Tuesday, my second presidential candidate had dropped out of the race. McGovern had won 21 Massachusetts delegates, though, including one "super-delegate" to be chosen at the Democratic State Convention. Being his highest-placed backer, I managed to win that seat and went to the National Democratic Convention after all.[57] And I got to go to San Francisco with a campaign I was actually much happier to be with than the one in my original plan. Teach me to wait and see if the field was really full before picking my candidate!

And the whole process only got more interesting, really. McGovern's 24 delegates, including three from Iowa, entitled him to a single seat on the platform committee. And the campaign was agreeable to letting me have that spot – I *was* their "highest ranking" delegate, after all. The party platform had already begun to decline in importance as the more entrepreneurial/less party-oriented presidential candidates started to prevail in the now more important primaries. There were, nonetheless, still battles to be fought, most of which would involve Hart delegates making motions that would inevitably fail when the late Paul Tully, who headed the Platform Committee team for the Mondale campaign which had the nomination wrapped up and therefore also had the votes to control the Platform Committee, would literally turn his thumb down on them in full view of the room, and turn it up on any Mondale-campaign approved amendments. The Mondale delegates generally voted according to the direction of Tully's thumb. The only real wild cards in the proceedings were the smaller Jesse Jackson delegation and the even-smaller McGovern delegation.

Although I had little idea of what to expect at a platform committee, I did understand that platforms had planks and I probably ought to think about bringing some with me. So I worked up three amendments, cleared them with the McGovern campaign, and offered them at a committee session. One was actually on a matter of some national controversy. It called for a law to require companies planning to close workplaces above a certain size to provide their employees with advance notice of their intent. The state-level version was my major piece of legislation in Massachusetts, but all of us involved in this effort ultimately wanted a national law. I would later learn that there had been a prior agreement on the part of the labor movement not to press for this proposal's inclusion in the party platform that year. It had actually been included in previous platforms but was to be jettisoned as part of the process of converting the document to a more generic, less potentially controversial statement of principles.

But since my proposals were not matters that had been in dispute between Mondale and Hart, the Mondale campaign had not prepared positions on them. The Mondale delegates looked to Tully's thumb, but Tully was showing them no thumb at all. The platform committee then proceeded to vote in favor of two of my amendments on the merits – a worker-ownership assistance initiative and the advance notice requirement. The labor delegates on the committee eagerly supported them, particularly the mandatory notice legislation. They hadn't broken their word. They had agreed not to introduce it, but voting against it when someone else introduced it was another thing. So the on-site Mondale campaign leadership thought they best not oppose it and, *voila,* it was back in the platform, for the last time, as it would turn

A Personal Introduction

out.

At the convention itself, the McGovern campaign attempted to deliver its handful of votes to Mondale in a show of party unity. Of course, none of us really wanted to do that and so a process of turning the votes around ensued, the prime argument being that we needed to show that McGovern was delivering on the pledge of support to Mondale that he had made after dropping out of the race. Shortly before the actual vote, they sent George's daughter Susan, whom I had come to know in the campaign, to try to persuade us remaining recalcitrants. Fearing that Susan was probably the one person capable to talking me out of my rejectionist stance at this point, I actually fled the Massachusetts delegation and hid out with some nearby state until almost the very moment of the vote. I had been led to understand that if just a couple of us were "off," it'd probably be okay, so I ducked back in the very end and voted for George, along with three other resisters.

Sticking with McGovern did relieve me of another problem. If I weren't going to vote for McGovern, I would have felt that my vote should go not to Mondale, but to Jackson who I actually thought was the next-best candidate. But while the 1984 Jackson campaign had great issues, this was also the not-quite-ready-for-prime-time Jackson who had just recently spoken of New York being a "Hymie town." So this was not a vote I was eager to make. As it turned out, I saw McGovern the following day and sought absolution and he did allow as how one needed to vote one's conscience – this had been the theme of his campaign, after all.

All in all, this experience kind of hooked me on presidential primaries as an opportunity for the right candidate to say what needed to be heard. And by 1988, Jesse Jackson had become a significantly better candidate, so this time around I had little hesitation in joining the campaign. My most memorable contribution was driving all over New Hampshire to speak at campaign house parties on Martin Luther King Day, when I discovered my love for presidential candidate surrogate speaking. And this time around, instead of running for a delegate slot myself, with delegate selection now having been shifted to after the primary, I opted to chair the caucus to pick the one Jackson

The Primary Route

delegate from our congressional district.

When Jackson opted against a third run in 1992, things sort of returned to normal on the presidential front. I ultimately signed on for the Tom Harkin campaign, feeling much as I had in 1983 with Cranston – that I viewed him as the best of a mainstream Democratic field, as opposed to a candidate with whom I agreed profoundly, as McGovern and Jackson had been. Nevertheless, I did surrogate campaign speaking and did make one trip to New Hampshire before Harkin dropped out fairly early on. And like most people, even on the left, I was barely aware of Larry Agran's campaign.

And then no challenger to incumbent President Bill Clinton in 1996 – not such a big surprise that. But the blandness of the 2000 Democratic campaign to succeed Clinton did come as something of surprise, or at least a disappointment, with the only challenge to incumbent Vice President Al Gore's quest for the top job coming from New Jersey Senator Bill Bradley who differed only ever so slightly. So with the Democrats seemingly locked into permanent middle-of-the-road continuity, I took the Ralph Nader third-party walk on the wild side. I even moved that the local San Francisco Democratic club I chaired endorse Nader. The motion failed by a single vote and when I delivered our club's official endorsement slate card supporting Gore to the doors of the neighborhood voters, I dropped off Nader literature with it.

My thinking on the Nader campaign was that it might be possible to build something sort of in the nooks and crannies of the electoral system. Which is to say that Gore was definitely going to win California and one of the quirks of the Electoral College system was that this meant that a substantial number of Californians could vote for Nader, make a statement about what the real issues ought to be in presidential election campaign and what they really thought, and maybe even organize something useful out of it. But it depended on people knowing how to vote tactically, meaning that if they fell into that group that thought that Nader was way preferable to Gore but really *did not want* Bush to win, they had to be made aware that there were some states where this meant you voted for Nader, as you wished to, and others where you were going to have to vote for Gore. And there was actually a considerable effort put into making that happen. Websites were set up to facilitate the pairing up of Gore voters from "runaway states" with Nader voters from states where the race was assumed to be close, although they were ultimately shut down by the government. I put a considerable effort into facilitating those match-ups among people I knew, as well – with little discernible success. The results, as we know, could not have been worse from the point of view of the voters described above: Bush wins and Nader gets blamed for it.

So when Dennis Kucinich announced his candidacy in 2004, I jumped at the chance to get involved. This looked like the first shot at bringing the big issues back into the presidential election, without an argument about how doing so would elect a Republican, since the second Jackson campaign sixteen years earlier. I had been aware of Kucinich since the early 1970s after a number of my friends had moved from Boston to Cleveland and become heavily involved in his administration when he was elected the city's "boy mayor" at age 31.

San Francisco has a lot of local Democratic Clubs, so I gave a lot of pitches for him at a lot of their meetings and at campaign house parties as well. And in California, I was back in a state with pre-primary candidate caucuses and once again won the top delegate spot in my congressional district. In fact, as he won his highest total in the state in that district, I actually came closer to being elected a Kucinich delegate than anyone else in California, but unfortunately even here he didn't quite crack fourteen percent and you need fifteen.

Obviously, the 2004 campaign had been no ringing success, yet Kucinich went out there again in 2008. So, putting aside my initial skepticism, after deciding that was non-productive, this time I went out and did the lion's share of the surrogate speaking for him throughout the entire Bay Area, instead of just in San Francisco. As it turned out I actually stayed in the race a bit longer than Kucinich himself, even. Having sworn off listening to broadcast news since back during the Gulf War, on the evening when I gave my last Kucinich pitch to a Democratic club, someone in the audience had to tell me that he had withdrawn from the race several hours earlier. Otherwise I wouldn't have known until I read the morning paper. Obviously I was eager for more, but that was going to have to wait for awhile. Much as I would have loved for someone to challenge Obama from the left in 2012, it did not happen – to nobody's great surprise.

So I wrote this book. And Bernie Sanders decided to run.

Acknowledgments

Thanks to Josh Freeman for reading the history chapters, to Michael Pincus for editing the whole thing, and to Kevin Moran for all his efforts. To Wikipedia, whose entries from the respective years constituted this book's principal sources of background information on the various years' presidential election campaigns. And to Jesse Jackson, Ralph Nader and Dennis Kucinich.

PHOTO CREDITS

Cover   White House in 1846; Library of Congress.

P   2   1972 campaign poster
P   18   Thomas J.O'Halloran, Library of Congress
P   22   totallyfreeimages.com/
P   38   1904 campaign poster
P   44   Library of Congress
P   49   Brown Brothers, Public domain
P   52   Kansas Historical Society
P   54   1892 campaign poster
P   57   Instituto Luiz Carlos Prestes
P   59   Library of Congress
P   61   Public domain
P   71   Library of Congress
P   80   rauscherpeter.wordpress.com
P   81   Independent Green Party of Virginia News
P   94   Truman Library
P   96   1952 campaign poster
P 104   1972 campaign poster
P 112   2004 campaign poster
P 116   Harper's Weekly, July 14, 1894
P 118   Library of Congress
P 132   Library of Congress
P 133   Public domain
P 135   Library of Congress
P 137   Library of Congress
P 138   Frank Wolfe; Creative Commons-ShareAlike
P 167   vitomarcantonioforum.com/

The Primary Route

Bibliography

James Bryce, *Modern Democracies, vol.2,* (New York: The MacMillan Company, 1921).

Robert Bussel, *From Harvard to the Ranks of Labor: Powers Hapgood and the American Working Class,* (University Park, PA: Pennsylvania State University Press, 1999).

Matthew A. Crenson, *Presidential Power Unchecked and Unbalanced,* (New York: Norton, 2007).

Donald Richard Deskins, Hanes Walton and Sherman C. Puckett, *Presidential Elections, 1789-2008: County, State, and National Mapping of...,* (Ann Arbor: University of Michigan Press, 2010).

Scott Farris, *Almost President: The Men Who Lost the Race but Changed the Nation,* (Guilford, Conn.: Lyons Press, 2012).

Charles L. Fontenay, *Estes Kefauver, A Biography,* (Knoxville: University of Tennessee Press, 1980).

Lawrence Goodwin, *The Populist Movement: A Short History of the Agrarian Revolt in America,* (New York: Oxford University Press, 1978).

David Halberstam, *The Fifties* (New York: Villard Books, 1993).

Steven F. Hayward, *The Age of Reagan: The Fall of the Old Liberal Order: 1964-1980,* (New York: Three Rivers Press, 2001).

William D. Haywood, *The Autobiography of Big Bill Haywood.* (New York: International Publishers, 1929).

William B. Hesseltine, *Third-party movements in the United States,* (Princeton, N.J.: Van Nostrand, 1962).

Bibliography

Robert Mann, *Wartime Dissent in America: A History and Anthology* (New York: Palgrave MacMillan, 2010).

Richard Michael Marano, *Vote your Conscience: The Last Campaign of George McGovern*, (Westport, Conn.: Praeger, 2003).

John R. McArthur, *You Can't Be President: The Outrageous Barriers to Democracy in America*, (New York: Melville House, 2008).

Bruce Miroff, *The Liberals' Moment: The McGovern Insurgency and the Identity Crisis of the Democratic Party*, (Lawrence : University Press of Kansas, 2007).

Norman Pollack, *The Populist Response to Industrial America*, (Cambridge: Harvard University Press, 1962).

Darcy G. Richardson, *Third Party Politics From the Nation's Founding to the Rise and Fall of the Greenback-Labor Party*, (New York : iUniverse, Inc., 2004)

Lance Selfa, *Democrats: A Critical History*, (Chicago: Haymarket Books, 2008).

L. Glen Seretan, *Daniel DeLeon, the Odyssey of An American Marxist*, (Cambridge, Mass., and London: Harvard University Press, 1979).

Micah Sifry, *Spoiling for a Fight*, (New York: Routledge, 2002).

Dwight Steward, Mr. Socialism: Norman Thomas – His Life an Times, (Secaucus, N.J.: L. Stuart, 1974).

Fred W. Thompson and Patrick Murfin, *The IWW: Its First Seventy Years*, (Chicago: Industrial Workers of the World, 1976).

T. Harry Williams, *Huey Long*, (Knopf, 876 pp.,1969).

The Primary Route

[1] The idea of "additive" political structures, as well as "subtractive" ones – such as the final presidential election – is elaborated in Chapter 3, *What Do We Know? Additive and Subtractive Political Systems.*

[2] Following Edward Snowden's revelations, we should perhaps not assume that the NSA isn't already scanning other planets itself.

[3] Brian Stelter, "Among Top News Stories, a War Is Missing," *New York Times*, 31 December 2012, B4.In the U.S., this has been standard practice for Democratic Party primary delegate lists since 1980, but there are, of course, no candidate lists in American elections for public office.

[4] Previously better known to the nation as Zelda on the Dobie Gillis Show.

[5] Theodore Roosevelt was the only candidate of what was considered a third party to finish as high as second. The incumbent Republican President William Howard Taft finished third with 23.2% and 8 electoral votes.

[6] Information on county level presidential vote throughout from *Presidential Elections, 1789-2008: County, State, and National Mapping of ...* by Donald Richard Deskins, Hanes Walton, Sherman C. Puckett.

[7] For more on the American Labor Party, see the section on fusion in Chapter 11.

[8] The other parties were Reform, Libertarian, Natural Law, Workers World, Constitution, Socialist and Socialist Workers.

[9] Coincidentally, the most prominent new left German student organization was also named SDS, although the initials stood not for Students for a Democratic Society, as they did in the U.S., but for Sozialistische Deutsche Studentenbund, or German Socialist Student League.

[10] In the U.S., this has been standard practice for Democratic Party primary delegate lists since 1980, but there are, of course, no candidate lists in American elections for public office.

[11] Individual candidates may win seats in German districts regardless of their party's overall performance, but a party will not receive the number of seats proportional to its share of the vote unless it reaches five percent of the national vote.

[12] Paul H. Giddens, "The Origin of the Direct Primary: The Crawford County System," The Western Pennsylvania Historical Magazine, Volume 60, Number 2, April 1977, 145-158.

[13] James Bryce, *Modern Democracies, vol.2*, (New York: The MacMillan Company, (1921), 130.

[14] The Socialist Party would even go the major parties one better when it chose its nominee, New York editor Allan Benson, in a nationwide mail-in vote, Debs having opted to pursue a congressional race in Indiana.

[15] David Halberstam, *The Fifties* (New York: Villard Books, 1993), 188.

Bibliography

[16] After winning his second nomination, Stevenson threw the vice presidential nomination open for the convention delegates to decide. Kefauver led on the first ballot, Massachusetts Senator John Kennedy passed him in the second, but Kefauver won it on the third.

[17] Speech to the U.S. Senate, September 1, 1970, Robert Mann, *Wartime Dissent in America: A History and Anthology* (New York: Palgrave MacMillan, 2010) 142.

[18] Steven F. Hayward, *The Age of Reagan: The Fall of the Old Liberal Order: 1964-1980*, New York, Random House, 2009) 344.

[19] Stephen Zunes, "George McGovern," *The Progressive,* 1 October, 1993.

[20] Associated Press, October 21, 1972.

[21] "Polls show big popularity loss for President," *Chicago Tribune*, August 16, 1973.

[22] John R. McArthur, *You Can't Be President: The Outrageous Barriers to Democracy in America,* (New York: Melville House, 2008), 56.

[23] Jesse Walker, "Five Faces of Jerry Brown," *The American Conservative*, 1 November, 2009

[24] LaRouche, who had previously been convicted of credit card fraud, asserted that rock and roll was created by British intelligence in order to subvert the United States and claimed to be the one who had inspired the Reagan administration's Strategic Defense Initiative, better known as "Star Wars." He had actually also won 5.4% of the 1996 primary vote against Clinton.

[25] Ford Fessenden and John M. Broder, "Study of Disputed Florida Ballots Finds Justices Did Not Cast the Deciding Vote," *New York Times*, November 12, 2001.

[26] Lance Selfa, *Democrats: A Critical History*, (Chicago: Haymarket Books, 2008) 244.

[27] Ibid., 220.

[28] Ibid., 5-6.

[29] *The Samuel Gompers Papers,* <http://www.gompers.umd.edu/quotes.htm>.

[30] Ibid.

[31] L. Glen Seretan, *Daniel DeLeon, the Odyssey of an American Marxist*, (Cambridge, Mass., and London: Harvard University Press), 150.

[32] William D. Haywood, *The Autobiography of Big Bill Haywood.* (New York: International Publishers, 1929), 171.

[33] Fred W. Thompson and Patrick Murfin, *The IWW: Its First Seventy Years*, (Chicago: Industrial Workers of the World, 1976), 10.

[34] Robert Bussel, *From Harvard to the Ranks of Labor: Powers Hapgood and the American Working Class,* (University Park, PA: the Pennsylvania State University Press, 1999) 106.

[35] The astute student of that obscure and byzantine structure by which we actually elect our presidents, known as the Electoral College, realizes that its rules require a majority vote to choose a president – but all of the fifty-one separate elections that choose those electors in the states and the District of Columbia are actually based upon winning a simple plurality in the various jurisdictions, with no possibilities for run-offs.

[36] Twenty years later, the Cleveland City Council recognized that his "courage and foresight" in rejecting the sale had saved the city nearly $200 million.

[37] All of the platform committee debates discussed here come from Democratic Party conventions, as this is where virtually all of the positions of interest to a modern reader of the left have been argued.

[38] Sam Tanenhaus, "The Power of Congress," *The New Yorker*, 19 January 2015, 72.

[39] The Bernie Sanders campaign has set up a website listing the systems in place in the various states.

[40] T. Harry Williams, *Huey Long*, (Knopf, 876 pp.,1969), 844.

[41] Micah Sifry, *Spoiling for a Fight*, (New York: Routledge, 2002), 279

[42] Ibid., 280. The New Party and the Working Families Party are discussed in the section on fusion in the next chapter.

[43] http://web.archive.org/web/20150126052026/http://www.gp.org/green-officeholders

[44] The other club was the Bernal Heights Democratic Club, which this writer served as president.

[45] While Libertarian Party candidates often hold foreign policy views consistent with those of the target audience of this book, their positions on domestic economic questions are generally antithetical and the party's activities therefore don't fall within the scope of this book. In 2015 the Libertarians claimed 144 local office holders in a range of different offices similar to that of the Greens.

[46] Angus King also serves in the U.S. Senate, having been elected as an independent from Maine. Unlike Sanders, King is something of a classical centrist with a political stance somewhere between that of most Republicans and most Democrats.

[47] The passage of the 17th Amendment to the Constitution formally transferred the power to elect U.S. Senators from the state legislatures to the voters in 1913.

[48] Peter Argesinger, "A Place on the Ballot: Fusion Politics and Antifusion Laws," *American Historical Review 287* (1980), p. 296.

[49] Sifry, *Spoiling for a Fight*, 230.

[50] http://web.archive.org/web/20150202230931/https://www.opensecrets.org/indu

[51] http://web.archive.org/web/20150202231532/https://www.opensecrets.org/lobby/indu s.php?id=P&year=2012

[52] http://web.archive.org/web/20150203201530/https://www.opensecrets.org/overview/

blio.php

The Center does note that "An important caveat must be added to these figures: "business" contributions from individuals are based on the donor's occupation/employer. Since nearly everyone works for someone, and since union affiliation is not listed on FEC reports, totals for business are somewhat overstated, while labor is understated. Still, the base of large individual donors is predominantly made up of business executives and professionals.

"Contributions under $200 are not included in these numbers, as they are not itemized."

[53]http://www.usatoday.com/story/news/politics/2015/01/26/koch-brothers-network-announces-889-million-budget-for-next-two-years/22363809/

[54]Afghanistan Study Group, AFL-CIO, American Medical Students Association, Americans for Democratic Action, Black Nurses Association, Blue Green Alliance, Campaign for America's Future, Campaign for Better Health Care, Campus Progress, Center for American Progress, Center for Budget and Policy Priorities, Center for Community Change, Center for International Policy, Center for Social Inclusion, Change to Win, Color of Change, Communications Workers of America, CREDO Action, Crooks & Liars, DailyKos, Democracy for America, DEMOS, Economic Policy Institute, Fenton Communications, Generational Alliance, Health Care for America Now, Herndon Alliance, Human Rights Watch, Institute for Policy Studies, Joint Center for Political and Economic Studies, Leadership Conference on Civil Rights, League of United Latin American Citizens, Media Matters for America, MoveOn.org, NAACP (National Association for the Advancement of Colored People), National Physicians Alliance, National Security Network, Netroots Nation, New Organizing Institute, Peace Action, People For the American Way Foundation, Progress Now, Progressive Change Campaign Committee, Scholars' Strategy Network, SEIU (Service Employees International Union), Sierra Club, Universal Health Care Action Network, US Action, WAND (Women's Action for Nuclear Disarmament), Wellstone Action, Westen Strategies, Win Without War

[55] *The Heights*, the student newspaper of my alma mater, Boston College, carried a story of an event that I don't particularly remember but must have made for a difficult day for me on that score. *The Heights* reported that I represented Cranston at a progressive endorsement gathering at which the McGovern spokesman said, "Cranston voted for and defends the B-1 Bomber while there is only one candidate calling for a 25 per-cent cut in military expenditures - that candidate is George McGovern."

[56] If Paul Sullivan – McGovern's 1984 campaign manager who promised to return my videotape of the Faneuil Hall event after he finished using it to make a campaign highlights film – is reading this, please send the tape back. It's not too late. (And could you send the highlights film, too, if it ever happened?)

[57] This was a dramatic turnabout for me in that a *Boston Globe* reporter had previously included me on a list of hidden primary losers. Delegate slots for the individual candidates had previously been chosen at congressional district-level caucuses. I had won the first male delegate slot at our Cranston caucus – but there would be no Cranston delegates.